Reading 英语趣味阅读系列

丛书主编　朱宾忠

行动的力量

The Power of Your Actions

主　编　吴　彩
副主编　徐玉军　陈枝蔚　金陈铭

WUHAN UNIVERSITY PRESS
武汉大学出版社

图书在版编目(CIP)数据

行动的力量/吴彩主编;徐玉军,陈枝蔚,金陈铭副主编. —武汉:武汉大学出版社,2012.7
英语趣味阅读系列/朱宾忠主编
ISBN 978-7-307-09517-5

Ⅰ.行… Ⅱ.①吴… ②徐… ③陈… ④金…
Ⅲ.英语—语言读物 Ⅳ.H319.4

中国版本图书馆 CIP 数据核字(2012)第 016297 号

封面图片为上海富昱特授权使用(ⓒ IMAGEMORE Co., Ltd.)

责任编辑:叶玲利　　责任校对:黄添生　　版式设计:韩闻锦

出版发行:武汉大学出版社　(430072　武昌　珞珈山)
　　　　　(电子邮件:wdp4@whu.edu.cn 网址:www.wdp.com.cn)
印刷:湖北恒泰印务有限公司
开本:950×1260　1/32　印张:7.5　字数:240千字　插页:1
版次:2012 年 7 月第 1 版　　2012 年 7 月第 1 次印刷
ISBN 978-7-307-09517-5/H·867　　定价:19.00 元

版权所有,不得翻印;凡购买我社的图书,如有缺页、倒页、脱页等质量问题,请与当地图书销售部门联系调换。

序言 PREFACE

兴趣是最好的老师。阅读兴趣是学生养成好的阅读习惯、提高阅读能力的核心要素之一。有兴趣阅读，学生才会在零碎时间中"见缝插针"地经常性阅读。众所周知，语言学习除了课堂教学材料（如课本和习题）以外还需要补充大量的课外阅读材料（报纸、杂志、故事、小说等）。一般而言，一个本族语学习者阅读课外材料的数量是课堂教学材料的十多倍甚至数十倍，这也正是人们能够掌握好本族语的最大保障。然而，中国学生在学习英语的过程中，除了课本和习题外，极少阅读其他英语读物。根据笔者2009年3月份针对3个省份（湖北、广东、福建）4座城市（武汉、丹江口、东莞、厦门）6所学校从初一到大一7个年级731名学生的问卷调查，除课本和习题外"从不"和"几乎不"看其他英文书籍的学生占46.03%，"偶尔"看的学生占51.60%，"经常"阅读的只有2.37%。

课本及习题是英语学习的主要素材，但仅限于课本及习题的多讲多练不足以大幅度提高阅读能力以及语言能力。学校英语课本的难度都高于多数学生自主阅读的语言水平，需要老师讲解后才能理解，而习题中的阅读部分差不多都是为考试服务的，无论是文章的编排形式还是篇幅的长短，一切都是"考试化"，如阅读理解、完形填空、短文改错等。很多练习阅读的习题集还会附上应付考试的技巧，以致许多学生见到阅读材料时脑子里想的只有两个字："答题"或"考试"。"阅读材料考试化"在较大程度上扼杀了学生的阅读兴趣，让他们不断体验英语学习中的"枯燥"和"疲劳"。也就是说，英语课本和习题不足以培养学生较浓厚的阅读兴趣，而缺乏阅读兴趣不利于养成好的阅读习惯，结果是课本中学到的词汇、短语、语法等知识也很少有机会在课外阅读中得到深化和保持。

什么样的英语故事更适合培养学生的阅读兴趣？25年来笔者在多座城市为近30所学校的中学生、大学生讲授或辅导过英语科目，也无数次因学生的请求频繁光顾书店搜寻适合他们阅读的英语故事。笔者发现，要培养学生的阅读兴趣，选择故事时需重点考虑以下因素：阅读的连续性、故事的趣味性、语言难度和汉语依赖性。

阅读的连续性。一口气把一个故事（或一本故事书）看完更容易享受阅读的乐趣。如果一边看故事，一边频繁地翻看词典、生词表或译文就不可避免地中断阅读的连续性，从而降低阅读兴趣。

故事的趣味性。阅读的连续性是人们欣赏故事、领悟语言的基本功，而故事的趣味性是吸引读者持续性阅读的最有效动力。上述问卷调查中74.41%的学生表示，他们挑选英文故事阅读时主要会考虑趣味性。

语言难度。语言难度是影响阅读的连续性和阅读兴趣的另一个重要因素，上述调查结果也表明了这一点：42.95%的学生挑选英文故事时主要会考虑语言难度；而"从不"和"几乎不"以及"偶尔"看其他英文书籍的学生当中，66.44%的学生认为他们读过的英文故事难度"太大"或"较大"，因而失去阅读的兴趣。所以，要保持学生的阅读兴趣，所选故事的难度最好是接近或略低于学校课本的语言程度。

汉语依赖性。许多学生阅读英语时习惯于一见到生词就查看词典（或生词表），有译文时先看译文。对汉语的过分依赖不仅影响到阅读的连续性，降低阅读兴趣，更不利于培养阅读英语的习惯。本丛书尝试把影响故事整体理解的词汇、短语、结构、语法、习俗等进行适当改写或在句中加上简明的汉字。比如，常见的被动语态对初学者是理解的难点，词典、词汇表和译文对此帮助不大，而三言两语的注释也解释不清，在句中加上简明的汉字反而简单有效。

"英语趣味阅读系列"丛书主要由武汉大学外语学院英文系教授（博导）朱宾忠博士、集美大学外语学院英语系副主任（副教授）黄明博士和广东东莞市高级中学高级教师吴彩担任主编，邀集了一批长期从事英语教学和研究的教师共同编写。丛书共四册，难度依次递进，内容各有侧重，共选编了500多个经典故事，分为童话故事、民间故事、情感故事、幽默故事四大类。所选故事趣味性强、语言地道、情节生动、真挚感人。本丛书在保持原文原汁原味的前提下对影响故事整体理解的难点部分进行了改写或添加简明的汉字，语言难度逐册提高，但力求让所有中学生、大学生在"无词典、无词表、无译文"的状态下一口气看完每一个完整的故事。本丛书的编写方式不仅降低了学生对汉语的依赖性，而且为阅读的连续性创造了条件。一口气看完本丛书中一个个动人故事也是学生真实体验"欣赏与自我欣赏"的一个新奇历程，即在欣赏优美英语故事的同时不知不觉开始欣赏自己英语水平的提高。总之，本丛书在提高学生阅读兴趣、养成英语阅读习惯、增强英语阅读信心、扩展英语文化知识、培养英语敏捷思维等方面将起到积极的推动作用。

黄 明

2012 年 6 月 1 日

于厦门集美大学白鹭湖畔

目录 CONTENTS

01. See How Much I Love You / 1
02. The Doll and the White Rose / 3
03. A Mother With Only One Eye / 6
04. For the Love of Mother / 8
05. The Golden Years / 10
06. A Touching Christmas Story / 12
07. The Toy / 15
08. Working Christmas Day / 18
09. The Late Love Story / 21
10. Best Teacher I Ever Had / 26
11. A Great Mistake / 28
12. You Are My Life / 29
13. Speak Out Your Love / 30
14. Unconditional Love / 32
15. Wind of Forgiveness / 34
16. So Much to Learn / 35
17. The Real Meaning of Peace / 36
18. I Will Always Be Around / 37
19. The Power of Your Actions / 39
20. Let Your Love Be Known / 42
21. I'll Always Be There for You / 44
22. If I Lose Honesty, I Won't Be Happy Forever / 46
23. Dating With a Second Woman / 48
24. A Love Story / 50

目录 CONTENTS

25. A True Gift of Love / 51
26. The Difference a Teacher Can Make / 52
27. A Brother Like That / 55
28. Family / 56
29. Love Is Just a Thread / 58
30. A Glass of Milk / 60
31. Paid in Full / 61
32. Hungry for Your Love / 63
33. You Are My Revenge / 67
34. A Gift of Love / 69
35. I Didn't Know How To Teach Until I Met You / 72
36. Interview with God / 75
37. The Blessed Dress / 76
38. Waiting at the Door / 79
39. Love and Time / 81
40. Gifts of Heart / 82
41. True Forgiveness / 85
42. The Little Girl Who Dared To Wish / 86
43. Puppies for Sale / 89
44. A Thanksgiving Story / 90
45. The Spirit of Santa Doesn't Wear a Red Suit / 93
46. A Guy Named Bill / 96
47. We Are Not Alone / 97
48. An Act of Kindness for a Broken Heart / 100

目录 CONTENTS

49. Thelma / 101
50. All Those Years / 102
51. The Smile / 103
52. Miles / 105
53. Broken Wing / 107
54. Playing Cupid / 109
55. The Plum Pretty Sister / 111
56. Daddy's Little Girl / 115
57. Is There Really a Prince Charming / 117
58. Scarecrow / 121
59. Love Letters / 125
60. There Are No Vans / 128
61. To Any Service Member / 131
62. The Santa Claus on the Highway / 133
63. The Fortune Cookie Prophecy / 137
64. A Coke and a Smile / 141
65. The Best Time of My Life / 144
66. The Easter Bunny / 145
67. Cyber Step-Mother / 146
68. The Pickle Jar / 148
69. Late for School / 151
70. Stepfather's Day / 155
71. Humor Them / 157
72. Who You Are Makes a Difference / 158

目录 CONTENTS

73. Jessie's Glove / 160
74. A Simple Act of Love / 161
75. My Highest Compliment / 164
76. Ronny's Book / 166
77. Writers in Prison / 169
78. Coffee Shop Kindness / 173
79. The Giving Trees / 176
80. The Last Straw / 177
81. Are You God? / 186
82. Timmy's Wish / 187
83. Win One for Me, Daddy / 190
84. A Surprise Gift for Mother / 192
85. Christmas Presence / 194
86. The Pillow / 197
87. A Lot of Bread / 199
88. Let Us Be United / 201
89. The Cat Lady / 205
90. For the Best / 206
91. Albert / 207
92. Christmas Roses / 209
93. Attitude Is Everything / 210
94. The Most Beautiful Flower / 213
95. He Never Missed a Game / 214
96. The House of 1,000 Mirrors / 217

目 录 **CONTENTS**

97. The Bridge Keeper	/ 218
98. A Goodbye Kiss	/ 219
99. The Baby Eagle Story	/ 221
100. The Unlocked Door	/ 224
参考文献	/ 226

01
See How Much I Love You

My grandparents were married for over half a century, and played their own special game from the time they had met each other. The goal of their game was to write the word "shmily" in a surprise place for the other to find. They took turns leaving "shmily" around the house, and as soon as one of them discovered it, it was their turn to hide it once more.

They dragged "shmily" with their fingers through the sugar and flour containers to await whoever was preparing the next meal. They **smeared**(涂抹)it in the dew on the windows overlooking the **patio**(露台)where my grandma always fed us warm, homemade pudding with blue food coloring. "Shmily" was written in the steam left on the mirror after a hot shower, where it would reappear bath after bath. At one point, my grandmother even unrolled an entire roll of toilet paper to leave "shmily" on the very last sheet. There was no end to the places "shmily" would **pop up**(突然出现). Little notes with "shmily" **scribbled**(潦草书写)hurriedly were found on dashboards and car seats, or taped to steering wheels. The notes were stuffed inside shoes and left under pillows. "Shmily" was written in the dust upon the

1

mantel(壁炉架) and traced in the ashes of the fireplace. This mysterious word was as much a part of my grandparents' house as the furniture.

It took me a long time before I was able to fully appreciate my grandparents' game. **Skepticism**(怀疑) has kept me from believing in true love—one that is pure and enduring. However, I never doubted my grandparents' relationship. It was more than their **flirtatious**(调情的) little games; it was a way of life. Their relationship was based on a devotion and passionate affection which not everyone is lucky to experience.

Grandma and Grandpa held hands every chance they could. They stole kisses as they bumped into each other in their tiny kitchen. They finished each other's sentences and shared the daily crossword puzzle and **word jumble**(字谜游戏). My grandma whispered to me about how cute my grandpa was, how handsome and old he had grown to be. She claimed that she really knew "how to pick 'em." Before every meal they bowed their heads and gave thanks, marveling at their blessings: a wonderful family, good fortune, and each other.

But there was a dark cloud in my grandparents' life: my grandmother had breast cancer. The disease had first appeared ten years earlier. As always, Grandpa was with her every step of the way. He comforted her in their yellow room, painted that way so that she could always be surrounded by sunshine, even when she was too sick to go outside.

Now the cancer was again attacking her body. With the help of a cane and my grandfather's steady hand, they went to church every morning. But my grandmother grew steadily weaker until, finally, she could not leave the house anymore. For a while, Grandpa would go to church alone, praying to God to watch over his wife. Then one day, what we all dreaded finally happened. Grandma was gone.

"Shmily." It was **scrawled**(潦草地写) in yellow on the pink ribbons of my grandmother's funeral **bouquet**(花束). As the crowd thinned and the last mourners turned to leave, my aunts, uncles,

cousins and other family members came forward and gathered around Grandma one last time. Grandpa stepped up to my grandmother's **casket**(棺材) and, taking a shaky breath, he began to sing to her. Through his tears and grief, the song came, a deep and throaty **lullaby** (摇篮曲). Shaking with my own sorrow, I will never forget that moment. For I knew that, although I couldn't begin to **fathom**(弄清楚) the depth of their love, I had been privileged to witness its unmatched beauty.

S-h-m-i-l-y: See How Much I Love You.

02

The Doll and the White Rose

I hurried into the local department store to grab some last minute Christmas gifts. I looked at all the people and **grumbled**(咕哝) to myself. I would be in here forever and I just had so much to do. Christmas was beginning to become such a **drag**(乏味的事情). I **kind of**(有点儿) wished that I could just sleep through Christmas. But I hurried the best I could through all the people to the toy department. Once again I kind of **mumbled**(咕哝) to myself at the prices of all these toys, and wondered if the grandkids would even play with them. I found myself in the doll aisle. Out of the corner of my eye I saw a little boy about five years old, who was holding a lovely doll.

He kept touching her hair and he held her so gently. I could not seem to help myself. I just kept looking over at the little boy and wondered who the doll was for. I watched him turn to a woman and he called his aunt by name and said, "Are you sure I don't have enough money?"

She replied a bit **impatiently**(不耐烦), "You know that you don't have enough money for it." The aunt told the little boy not to go anywhere. She said that she had to go and get some other things and would be back in a few minutes. And then she left the aisle. The boy continued to hold the doll. After a bit I asked the boy who the doll was for.

"It is the doll my sister wanted so badly for Christmas," said the boy. "She just knew that Santa would bring it."

I told him that maybe **Santa Claus**(圣诞老人)was going to bring it. He said, "No, Santa can't go where my sister is. I have to give the doll to my Mama to take to her."

I asked him where his sister was. He looked at me with the saddest eyes and said, "She was gone to be with **Jesus**(耶稣). My Daddy says that Mama is going to have to go to be with her."

My heart nearly stopped beating. Then the boy looked at me again and said, "I told my Daddy to tell my Mama not to go yet. I told him to tell her to wait till I got back from the store."

Then he asked me if I wanted to see his picture. I told him I'd love to. He pulled out some picture he had taken at the front of the store. He said, "I want my Mama to take this with her so she doesn't ever forget me. I love my Mama so much and I wish she would not have to leave me. But Daddy says she will need to be with my sister."

I saw that the little boy had lowered his head and had grown so quiet. While he was not looking, I reached into my purse and got out a handful of **bills**(钞票).

"Shall we count that money one more time?" I asked the little boy.

He grew excited and said, "Yes, I just know it has to be enough." So I slipped my money in with his and we began to count it. Of course it was plenty for the doll. He softly said, "Thank you Jesus for giving me enough money." Then the boy said to me, "I just asked Jesus to give me enough money to buy this doll so Mama can take it with her to give my sister. And he heard my prayer. I wanted to ask him for enough to buy my Mama a white rose, but I didn't ask him.

Now he gave me enough to buy the doll and a rose for my Mama. She loves white rose so much."

In a few minutes the aunt came back and I wheeled my cart away.

I could not keep from thinking about the little boy as I finished my shopping in a totally different spirit than when I had started. And I kept remembering a story I had seen in the newspaper several days earlier about a drunk driver hitting a car and killing a little girl and the Mother was in serious condition. The family was deciding on whether to **remove the life support**(拿掉吸氧机). Now surely this little boy did not belong with that story.

Two days later I read in the paper where the family had disconnected the life support and the young woman had died. I could not forget the little boy and just kept wondering if the two were somehow connected. Later that day, I could not help myself and I went out and bought some white roses and took them to the funeral home where the young woman was. And there she was, holding a lovely white rose, the beautiful doll, and the picture of the little boy in the store. I left there in tears. Their life changed forever. The love that little boy had for his little sister and his mother was overwhelmed. And in a split second a drunk driver had ripped the life of that little boy to pieces.

03

A Mother with Only One Eye

My Mom only had one eye. I hated her—she was such an **embarrassment**(令人难堪的人). My Mom ran a small shop at a **flea market**(跳蚤市场). She collected little **weeds**(废品) and such to sell—anything for the money we needed. She was such an embarrassment.

There was this one day during elementary school. I remember that it was field day, and my Mom came. I was so embarrassed. How could she do this to me? I threw her a hateful look and ran out. The next day at school many students laughed at me, "Your Mom only has one eye?!"

I wished that my Mom would just disappear from this world so I said to my Mom, "Mom, why don't you have the other eye?! You're only going to make me a laughingstock. Why don't you just die?"

My Mom did not respond. I guess I felt a little bad, but at the same time, it felt good to think that I had said what I'd wanted to say all this time. Maybe it was because my Mom hadn't punished me, I didn't think that I had hurt her feelings very badly.

That night, I woke up and went to the kitchen to get a glass of

water. My Mom was crying there, so quietly, as if she was afraid that she might wake me. I took a look at her, and then turned away.

Because of the thing I had said to her earlier, there was something pinching at me in the corner of my heart. Even so, I hated my mother who was crying out of her one eye. So I told myself that I would grow up and become successful, because I hated my one-eyed mother and our **desperate poverty**(赤贫).

Then I studied really hard. I left my mother and came to **Seoul**(首尔) and studied, and got accepted in the Seoul University with all the confidence I had. Then, I got married. I bought a house of my own. Then I had kids, too.

Now I'm living happily as a successful man. I like it here because it's a place that doesn't remind me of my Mom. This happiness was getting bigger and bigger, when someone unexpected came to see me.

"What?! Who's this?!" It was my mother—still with her one eye. I felt as if the whole sky was falling apart on me. My little girl ran away, scared of my Mom's eye.

And I asked her, "Who are you? I don't know you!!!" as if I tried to make that real. I screamed at her, "How dare you come to my house and scare my daughter! GET OUT OF HERE! NOW!"

And to this, my mother quietly answered, "Oh, I'm so sorry. I may have gotten the wrong address."

Soon she went away from my house. Thank goodness—she doesn't recognize me. I was quite relieved. I told myself that I wasn't going to care, or think about this for the rest of my life.

Then a wave of relief came upon me. One day, a letter regarding a school reunion came to my house. I lied to my wife saying that I was going on a business trip.

After the reunion, I went down to the old shack that I used to call a house—just out of curiosity there. I found my mother fallen on the cold ground. But I did not shed a single tear. She had a piece of paper in her hand—it was a letter to me.

She wrote:

My son, I think my life has been long enough now. And I won't visit Seoul any more, but would it be too much to ask if I wanted you to come visit me once in a while? I miss you so much. And I was so glad when I heard you were coming for the reunion. But I decided not to go to the school—for you. I'm sorry that I only have one eye, and I was an embarrassment for you. You see, when you were very little, you got into an accident, and lost your eye. As a mother, I couldn't stand watching you having to grow up with only one eye, so I gave you mine. I was so proud of my son that was seeing a whole new world for me, in my place, with that eye. I was never upset at you for anything you did—the couple times that you were angry with me. I thought to myself, "It's because he loves me." I miss the times when you were still young around me. I miss you so much. I love you. You mean the world to me.

My world shattered! Then I cried for the person who lived for me—MY MOTHER.

For the Love of Mother

When William—a 10-year-old boy and somewhat **scruffy-looking** (衣着不整齐的), enrolled himself to learn the piano, the music teacher was **reluctant** (勉强的) to accept him. She preferred her students to start their music lessons at a younger age when their fingers are nimble.

"William, why do you want to learn the piano?" the teacher asked.

"I want to play for my mother."

The teacher noticed the tears in the boy's eyes as he answered her.

She had no heart to turn him down and accepted William as her student. But at each music lesson, William appeared to be in a hurry and played badly.

"My mother is waiting outside for me," he would tell the teacher.

The teacher was tempted to advise William not to waste his time as he never hit the right note. But there was something about William, which she was fascinated with the tender look of his eyes each time he mentioned "mother".

Suddenly, William stopped coming for his lessons. At the end of the semester year, the music teacher decided to organize a piano **recital**(独奏会) for her students. She was surprised to find William's application that he would like to contribute a musical piece.

The day came and William appeared with his hair uncombed and his shirt **creased**(褶皱的). When it was his turn to play, he bowed and said, "Tonight I'm dedicating my music to my mother." As he sat down and put his fingers on the keyboard, the most beautiful sound of music was heard. Everyone later asked why he didn't bring his mother as she would surely be proud to hear him play.

William replied, "My mother was **stone deaf**(完全聋的) and she could never hear my play during her life time. Yet she sacrificed her time and money to let me learn the piano. This morning mother passed away. I'm sure she is now happy as she can hear my piano recital. I chose a piece from Beethoven's **concerto**(协奏曲). As you all know, Beethoven was **submerged**(陷入) with deafness at the triumph of his career. The piece symbolized his struggle for freedom from tyranny and released him from darkness, and so was mother."

Everyone was electrified to hear what William said and tears welled over their eyes.

The music teacher came to **embrace**(拥抱) him and proudly exclaimed, "William, not only your mother but we all are proud of you. We are deeply touched by your devotion and your love for mother."

05

The Golden Years

My best friend, Cocoa, and I live in a senior-citizen apartment in a lovely small town. Cocoa is a ten-year-old **poodle**(卷毛小狗) and I am a sixty-nine-year-old lady, so you can see we both qualify as senior citizens.

Years ago, I promised myself that when I retired I would get a chocolate poodle to share my golden years. From the very first, Cocoa has always been exceptionally well-behaved. I never have to tell him anything more than once. He was **housebroken**(管教好的) and has never done anything naughty. He is extremely neat. When taking toys from his box to play, he always puts them back when he is finished. I have been accused of being obsessively neat, and sometimes I wonder if he **mimics**(模仿) me or if he was born that way, too.

He is a wonderful companion. When I throw a ball for him, he picks it up in his mouth and throws it back to me. We sometimes play a game I played as a child—but never with a dog. He puts his paw on my hand, I cover it with my other hand, he puts his paw on top, and I slide my hand out from underneath the pile and lay it on top, and so on. He does many amusing things that make me laugh, and when that

happens, he is so delighted. He just keeps it up. I enjoy his company immensely.

But almost two years ago, Cocoa did something strange. Was it a miracle or a **coincidence**(巧合)? It is certainly a mystery.

One afternoon, Cocoa started acting strangely. I was sitting on the floor playing with him when he started pawing and sniffing at the right side of my chest. He had never done anything like this ever before, and I told him, "No." With Cocoa, one "no" is usually enough, but not that day. He stopped briefly, then suddenly ran toward me from the other side of the room, throwing his entire weight—eighteen pounds—at the right side of my chest. He crashed into me and I yelped in pain. It hurt more than I thought it should have.

Soon after this, I felt a **lump**(肿块). I went to my doctors, and after X-rays, tests and lab work were done, they told me I had cancer.

When cancer starts, for an unknown reason, a wall of **calcium** (钙) builds. Then the lump or cancer attaches itself to this wall. When Cocoa jumped on me, the force of the impact broke the lump away from the calcium wall. This made it possible for me to notice the lump. Before that, I couldn't see it or feel it, so there was no way for me to know it was there.

I had a complete **mastectomy**(乳房切除术) and the cancer has not spread to any other part of my body. The doctors told me if the cancer had gone **undetected**(未被发现) even six more months, it would have been too late.

Was Cocoa aware of just what he was doing? I'll never really know. What I do know is that I'm glad I made a promise to spend my golden years with this wonderful chocolate brown poodle—for Cocoa not only shares his life with me, he has made sure that I will be around to share my life with him!

06

A Touching Christmas Story

For many of us, one Christmas stands out from all the others, the one when the meaning of the day shone clearest. My own "truest" Christmas began on a rainy spring day in the **bleakest**(暗淡的) of my life.

Recently **divorced**(离婚的), I was in my 20s. I had no job and was on my way downtown to go the rounds of the employment offices. I had no umbrella, for my old one had **fallen apart**(散了架), and I could not afford another one.

I sat down in the streetcar and there against the seat was a beautiful silk umbrella with a silver handle **inlaid**(镶嵌着) with gold and necks of bright **enamel**(珐琅). I had never seen anything so lovely.

I examined the handle and saw a name engraved among the golden **scrolls**(卷轴). The usual procedure would have been to turn in the umbrella to the conductor, but **on impulse**(一时冲动) I decided to take it with me and find the owner myself.

I got off the streetcar in a **downpour**(瓢泼大雨) and thankfully opened the umbrella to protect myself. Then I searched a telephone book for the name on the umbrella and found it. I called and a lady

answered.

Yes, she said in surprise, that was her umbrella, which her parents, now dead, had given her for a birthday present. But, she added, it had been stolen from her **locker**(衣帽柜) at school (she was a teacher) more than a year before.

She was so excited that I forgot I was looking for a job and went directly to her small house. She took the umbrella, and her eyes filled with tears.

The teacher wanted to give me a reward, but, though twenty dollars was all I had in the world, her happiness at **retrieving**(重新找到) this special possession was such that to have accepted money would have spoiled something. We talked for a while, and I must have given her my address. I don't remember.

The next six months were **wretched**(不幸的). I was able to obtain only temporary employment here and there, for a small salary. But I put aside twenty-five or fifty cents when I could afford it for my little girl's Christmas presents.

My last job ended the day before Christmas, my thirty-dollar rent was soon due, and I had fifteen dollars to my name, which Peggy and I would need for food.

She was home from the boarding school and was excitedly looking forward to her gift next day, which I had already bought. I had bought her a small tree, and we were going to decorate it that night.

The air was full of the sound of Christmas merriment as I walked from the streetcar to my small apartment. Bells rang and children shouted in the bitter dusk of the evening, and windows were lighted and everyone was running and laughing. But there should be no Christmas for me, I knew, no gifts, no remembrance whatever.

As I struggled through the snowdrifts, I had just about reached the lowest point in my life. Unless a miracle happened, I would be homeless in January, foodless, jobless. I had prayed steadily for weeks, and there had been no answer but this coldness and darkness, this harsh air, this **abandonment**(遗弃). God and men had completely forgotten me. I felt so helpless and so lonely. What was to become of us?

I looked in my mail box. There were only **bills**(账单) in it, a sheaf of them, and two white envelopes which I was sure contained more bills. I went up three dusty flights of stairs and I cried, shivering in my thin coat.

But I made myself smile so I could greet my little daughter with a pretense of happiness. She opened the door for me and threw herself in my arms, screaming joyously and demanding that we decorate the tree immediately.

Peggy had proudly set our kitchen table for our evening meal and put pans out and three cans of food which would be our dinner. For some reason, when I looked at those pans and cans, I felt broken-hearted. We would have only hamburgers for our Christmas dinner tomorrow.

I stood in the cold little kitchen, misery overwhelmed me. For the first time in my life, I doubted the existence of God and His mercy, and the coldness in my heart was colder than ice.

The doorbell rang and Peggy ran fleetly to answer it, calling that it must be Santa Claus. Then I heard a man talking heartily to her and went to the door. He was a delivery man, and his arms were full of parcels. "This is a mistake," I said, but he read the name on the parcels and they were for me.

When he had gone, I could only stare at the boxes. Peggy and I sat on the floor and opened them. A huge doll, three times the size of the one I had bought for her. Gloves. Candy. A beautiful leather purse. Incredible! I looked for the name of the sender. It was the teacher, the address was simply "California", where she had moved.

Our dinner the night was the most delicious I had ever eaten. I forgot I had no money for the rent and only fifteen dollars in my purse and no job. My child and I ate and laughed together in happiness.

Then we decorated the little tree and marveled at it. I put Peggy to bed and set up her gifts around the tree and a sweet peace flooded me like a **benediction**(祝福). I had some hope again. I could even examine the sheaf of bills without **cringing**(畏缩).

07

The Toy

It was 1952 and my father was away at war, leaving my mother and me behind to face hardship alone. I was only ten years old then. My mother was a **surgeon**(外科医生) and worked at the local clinic a few blocks from where we lived. We both **resided**(住) in an old apartment in the city. It was noisy and cold in the winter, whereas **humid**(潮湿) in the summer. My mother argued with the landlord constantly, as did the other **tenants**(房客). To their dismay, the landlord made promises, which he never kept. My mother's only revenge for this devil was that he would burn in hell someday. I learned a valuable lesson that year which carries on to this day.

The bell rang and thoughts of Christmas were the only thing on my mind. I raced home from school in the fresh snow that fell while I was in school. It lay there on the ground, white and smooth, waiting for my boots to disturb its beauty. I stopped briefly to gather some snow in my hands, packing it tight, then I threw it at Susie as I ran past her.

"Danny, I'm telling your mother on you," she cried. I laughed and ran away.

The five-story building where I lived was made of brown bricks.

15

There was a large, **cement stoop**(水泥台阶) in front of the building as you entered. A **spiral**(螺旋形) staircase reached up to our apartment and continued to the top of the building. At the very top of the steps was a door that led you to the **terrace**(楼顶平台). The summer brought many parties up there. Sometimes I would go up there and watch old man Macinni tending to his pigeons.

The apartment was empty when I arrived and a note was attached to the refrigerator. My mother was **working a double shift**(加班) and left me instructions for the day. I became angry and ripped the note in several pieces. We had planned on making Christmas biscuits and apple pies together, but my mother spoiled it by working.

I was angry for several minutes, and then realized I was alone. My mother hid the Christmas presents somewhere in her bedroom and I found this to be the perfect opportunity to investigate. I carefully **rummaged**(翻找) through her closet, finding most of the gifts wrapped in linen cloth. All but one toy, a model airplane.

I took the airplane to the living room and played with it for a long time. I was still mad at my mother and I **hurled**(猛掷) the airplane into the air. It was so **crisp**(脆的) and crashed down on the floor, breaking one of its wings.

I stood frozen with my eyes and mouth wide open, staring down at the plane. Oh boy, am I in trouble! Picking up the broken parts of the plane, I thought, how was I going to explain this? I had not got even a coin in my pocket. Where did my mother buy the plane? How can I make some money to replace it? Who would give me a job now? On Christmas Eve! Then I heard my mother coming through the door. This is awful! Why was she coming home now? I raced to my room, hiding the broken plane under my sweater.

"Danny?"

"Yeah, Mom?"

"I came home to take a present to one of my patients," she shouted back at me.

I sat on my bed, unable to come up with a good explanation for

the toy missing in her closet. The silence was **torture**(折磨). I did not hear my mother asking herself, where did that toy go? Or yell for me to come in her room. All I heard was a gentle knock on my door. I slowly went to the door and opened it. My mother stood there, leaning against the doorframe with her arms folded in front of her. She stared at the lump that **protruded**(突出) from my belly.

After telling my mother the horrible truth, she made me put my coat on and told me to follow her. We left bowed down as we walked. The street was **illuminated**(照亮) with Christmas lights. People busied the streets with their arms full of packages. I thought they all were staring at me for the terrible thing I had done. I knew why my mother was taking me to where she worked. The county clinic bore many tales.

Climbing the steps without catching our breath, we entered the clinic. We climbed more steps and reached the floor where my mother worked. Several nurses my mother knew greeted us with a "Merry Christmas". My mother returned the greetings without stopping as we continued down a lobby. We stopped outside a **ward**(病房) and I peeked inside the dim ward. There in a bed was a boy who looked very sick.

"That boy is going to die, Danny," my mother told me. "Possibly today, maybe tomorrow. He loves planes. I knew his mother could not afford to buy him one. So I did. I count my blessings every night and think of this boy and how grateful I am that you are not in that bed."

The words cut hard and sharp in my heart. The tears rolled down my face and I was so guilty. I ran as fast as I could, down the lobby and out of the clinic. I ran home and into my room where I cried myself to sleep.

Nowadays, 30 years have passed. I am sitting behind my desk at my electronic enterprise, waiting for my wife. Susie and I married when we graduated from high school. On every Christmas Eve, Susie and I take toys for the little children at the local **shelters**(避难所). **Hitherto**(到目前为止), we have never missed this seasonal tradition.

08

Working Christmas Day

It was an unusually quiet day in the **emergency**(急诊) room on December twenty-fifth. Quiet, that is, except for the nurses who were standing around the nurses' station grumbling about having to work Christmas Day.

I had just been out to the waiting room to clean up. Since there were no patients waiting to be seen at the time, I came back to the nurses' station for a cup of hot **cider**(苹果汁) from the **crockpot**(电炖锅) someone had brought in for Christmas. Just then an admitting clerk came back and told me I had five patients waiting to be evaluated.

I **whined**(抱怨道), "Five, how did I get five? I was just out there and no one was in the waiting room."

"Well, there are five signed in." So I went straight out and called the first name. Five bodies showed up at my desk, a pale **petite**(娇小的) woman and four small children in somewhat **rumpled**(皱的) clothing.

"Are you all sick?" I asked suspiciously.

"Yes," she said weakly, and lowered her head.

"Okay," I replied, unconvinced, "who's first?" One by one they

sat down, and I asked the usual **preliminary**(初步的) questions. When it came to descriptions of their problems, things got a little **vague**(含糊). Two of the children had headaches, but the headaches weren't accompanied by the normal body language of holding the head or trying to keep it still. Two children had earaches, but only one could tell me which ear was affected. The mother complained of a cough, but seemed to work to produce it.

Something was wrong with the picture. Our hospital policy, however, was not to turn away any patient, so we would see them. When I explained to the mother that it might be a little while before a doctor saw her because, even though the waiting room was empty, **ambulances**(救护车) had brought in several, more critical patients, in the back, she responded, "Take your time, it's warm in here." She turned and, with a smile, guided her children into the waiting room.

On a hunch(凭直觉)(call it nursing judgment), I checked the chart after the admitting clerk had finished registering the family. No address—they were homeless. The waiting room was warm.

I looked out at the family huddled by the Christmas tree. The littlest one was pointing at the television and exclaiming something to her mother. The oldest one was looking at her reflection in an **ornament**(装饰品) on the Christmas tree.

I went back to the nurses' station and mentioned we had a homeless family in the waiting room—a mother and four children between four and ten years of age. The nurses, grumbling about working Christmas, turned to **compassion**(同情) for a family just trying to get warm on Christmas. The team went into action, much as we do when there's a medical emergency. But this one was a Christmas emergency.

We were all offered a free meal in the hospital **cafeteria**(餐厅) on Christmas Day, so we claimed that meal and prepared a **banquet**(宴会) for our Christmas guests.

We needed presents. We put together oranges and apples in a basket one of our **vendors**(小贩) had brought to the department for

19

Christmas. We made little bags of stickers we borrowed from the X-ray department, candy that one of the doctors had brought to the nurses, **crayons**(蜡笔) the hospital had from a recent coloring contest, nurse bear buttons the hospital had given to the nurses at annual training day and little fuzzy bears that nurses clipped onto their **stethoscopes**(听诊器). We also found a mug, a package of powdered cocoa, and a few other **odds and ends**(零碎的东西). We pulled **ribbon**(丝带) and wrapping paper and bells off the department's decorations that we had all contributed to. As seriously as we met physical needs of the patients that came to us that day, our team worked to meet the needs, and **exceed**(超过) the expectations, of a family who just wanted to be warm on Christmas Day.

We took turns joining the Christmas party in the waiting room. Each nurse took his or her lunch break with the family, choosing to spend their "off duty" time with these people whose laughter and delightful chatter became quite **contagious**(有感染力的). When it was my turn, I sat with them at the little banquet table we had created in the waiting room. We talked for a while about dreams. The four children were telling me about what they would like to be when they grow up. The six-year-old started the conversation. "I want to be a nurse and help people," she declared.

After the four children had shared their dreams, I looked at the Mom. She smiled and said, "I just want my family to be safe, warm and content—just like they are right now."

The "party" lasted most of the shift, before we were able to locate a shelter that would take the family in on Christmas Day. The mother had asked that their charts be pulled, so these patients were not seen that day in the emergency department. But they were treated.

As they walked to the door to leave, the four-year-old came running back, gave me a hug and whispered, "Thanks for being our angels today." As she ran back to join her family, they all waved one more time before the door closed. I turned around slowly to get back to work, a little embarrassed for the tears in my eyes. There stood a

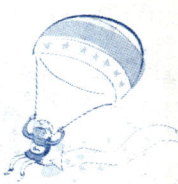

group of my coworkers, one with a box of **tissues**(纸巾), which she passed around to each nurse who worked a Christmas Day she will never forget.

09
The Late Love Story

I was always a little **in awe**(敬畏) of Great-aunt Stephina Roos. Indeed, as children we were all frankly terrified of her. The fact that she did not live with the family, preferring her tiny cottage and **solitude**(独居) to the comfortable but rather noisy household where we were brought up, added to the respectful fear in which she was held.

We used to take it in turn to carry small **delicacies**(美食) which my mother had made down from the big house to the little cottage where Great-aunt Stephina and an old colored maid spent their days. Old Tante Sanna would open the door to the rather frightened little messenger and would usher him or her into the dark dwelling, where the **shutters**(百叶窗) were always closed to keep out the heat and the flies. There we would wait, trembling but not altogether unpleasant.

She was a tiny little woman to inspire so much **veneration**(崇拜). She was always dressed in black, and her dark clothes melted into the shadows of the house and made her look smaller than ever. But you felt the moment she entered that something important and strong had come in with her, although she moved slowly, and her voice was sweet and soft.

She never embraced us. She would greet us and take out hot little hands in her own beautiful cool one, with blue **veins**(血管) standing out on the back of it, as though the white skin were almost too

delicate(脆弱) to contain them.

Tante Sanna would bring in dishes of sweet, sticky candy, or a great bowl of grapes or peaches, and Great-aunt Stephina would talk mostly about happenings on the farm, and, more rarely, of the outer world.

When we had finished our sweetmeats or fruit, she would accompany us to the **stoep**(门廊), asking us to thank our mother for her gift and sending old-fashioned messages to her and the father. Then she would turn and enter the house, closing the door behind, so that it became once more a place of mystery.

As I grew older I found, rather to my surprise, that I had become really fond of my old great-aunt. But to this day I do not know what strange **impulse**(冲动) made me take George to see her and to tell her, before I had **confided in**(告诉……秘密) another living soul, of our **engagement**(婚约). To my astonishment, she was delighted.

"An Englishman," she exclaimed. "But that is splendid, splendid. And you," she turned to George, "you are making your home in this country? You do not intend to return to England just yet?"

She seemed **relieved**(放心) when she heard that George had bought a farm near our own farm and intended to settle in South Africa. She became quite **animated**(兴致勃勃的), and chattered away to him.

After that I would often slip away to the little cottage. Once she was somewhat disappointed on hearing that we had decided to wait for two years before getting married, but when she learned that my father and mother were both pleased with the match she seemed **reassured** (感到放心).

Still, she often appeared anxious about my love affair, and would ask questions that seemed to me strange, almost as though she feared that something would happen to destroy my romance. But I was quite unprepared for her outburst when I mentioned that George thought of paying a short visit to England before we were married.

"He must not do it," she cried. "Ina, you must not let him go.

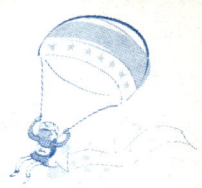

Promise me you will prevent him."

When she said this, she was trembling all over. I did what I could to **console**(安慰) her, but she looked so tired and pale that I persuaded her to go to her room and rest, promising to return the next day.

When I arrived, I found her sitting on the stoep. She looked lonely and **pathetic**(可怜的). For the first time I wondered why no man had ever taken her and looked after her and loved her. Mother had told me that Great-aunt Stephina had been lovely as a young girl, and although no trace of that beauty remained, except perhaps in her brown eyes, yet she looked so small and appealing that any man, one felt, would have wanted to protect her.

She paused, as though she did not quite know how to begin.

Then she seemed to give herself, mentally, a little shake. "You must have wondered," she said, "why I was so upset at the thought of young George's going to England without you. I am an old woman, and perhaps I have the silly **fancies**(幻想) of the old, but I should like to tell you my own love story, and then you can decide whether it is wise for your man to leave you before you are married."

"I was quite a young girl when I first met Richard Weston. He was an Englishman who boarded with the Van Rensburgs on the next farm, four or five miles from us. Richard was not strong. He had a weak chest, and the doctors had sent him to South Africa so that the dry air could cure him. He taught the Van Rensburg children, who were younger than I was, but he did this for pleasure and not because he needed money.

"We loved each other from the first moment we met, though we did not speak of our love until the evening of my eighteenth birthday. All our friends and relatives had come to my party, and in the evening we danced on the big old carpet which we had laid down in the barn. Richard had come with the Van Rensburgs, and we danced together as often as we dared, which was not very often, for my father hated the **Uitlanders**(南非的外国人). Indeed, for a time he had quarrelled with Mynheer Van Rensburg for allowing Richard to board with him, but

23

afterwards he got used to the idea, and was always polite to the Englishman, though he never liked him.

"That was the happiest birthday of my life, for while we were resting between dances Richard took me outside into the cool, moonlit night. There, under the stars, he told me he loved me and asked me to marry him. Of course I promised I would, for I was too happy to think of what my parents would say, or indeed of anything except Richard was not at our meeting place as he had arranged. I was disappointed but not alarmed, for so many things could happen to either of us to prevent us from keeping our **tryst**(约会). I thought that next time we visited the Van Ransburgs, I should hear what had kept him and we could plan further meetings.

"So when my father asked if I would drive with him to Driefontein, I was delighted. But when we reached the homestead and were sitting on the stoep drinking our coffee, we heard that Richard had left quite suddenly and had gone back to England. His father had died, and now he was the **heir**(继承人) and must go back to look after his **estates**(遗产).

"I do not remember very much more about that day, except that the sun seemed to have stopped shining and the country no longer looked beautiful and full of promise, but **bleak**(凄凉的) and **desolate**(阴郁的) as it sometimes does in winter or in times of drought. Late that afternoon, Jantje, the little Hottentot herd boy, came up to me and handed me a letter, which he said the English boss had left for me. It was the only love letter I ever received, but it turned all my bitterness and grief into a peacefulness which was the nearest I could get, then, to happiness. I knew Richard still loved me, and somehow, as long as I had his letter, I felt that we could never be really parted, even if he were in England and I had to remain on the farm. I have it yet, and though I am an old, tired woman, it still gives me hope and courage."

"It must have been a wonderful letter, Aunt Stephina," I said.

The old lady came back from her dreams of that far-off romance.

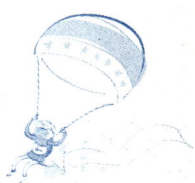

"Perhaps," she said, hesitating a little, "perhaps, my dear, you would care to read it?"

"I should love to, Aunt Stephina," I said gently.

She rose at once and tripped into the house as eagerly as a young girl. When she came back, she handed me a letter. Faded and yellow with age, the edges of the envelope were worn and **frayed**(磨破) as though it had been much handled. But when I came to open it, I found that the **seal**(封口) was unbroken.

"Open it, open it," said Great-aunt Stephina, and her voice was shaking.

I broke the seal and read.

It was not a love letter in the true sense of the word, but pages of the **minutest**(详细的) **directions**(说明) of how "my sweetest Stephina" was to **elude**(躲避) her father's **vigilance**(警戒), creep down to the drift at night and there meet Jantje with a horse which would take her to Smitsdorp. There she was to go to "my true friend, Henry Wilson", who would give her money and make arrangements for her to follow her lover to Cape Town and from there to England, "where, my love, we can be married at once. But if, my dearest, you are not sure that you can face life with me in a land strange to you, then do not take this important step, for I love you too much to wish you the smallest unhappiness. If you do not come, and if I do not hear from you, then I shall know that you could never be happy so far from the people and the country which you love. If, however, you feel you can keep your promise to me, but are too afraid of a journey to England unaccompanied, then write to me, and I will, by some means, return to fetch my bride."

I read no further.

"But Aunt Stephina!" I **gasped**(喘气说). "Why...why...?"

The old lady was watching me with trembling eagerness, her face flushed and her eyes bright with expectation.

"Read it aloud, my dear," she said. "I want to hear every word of it. There was never anyone I could trust...Uitlanders were hated in my young days...I could not ask anyone."

"But, Auntie, don't you even know what he wrote?"

The old lady looked down, troubled and shy like a child who has **unwittingly**(无意中) done wrong.

"No, dear," she said, speaking very low. "You see, I never learned to read."

10

Best Teacher I Ever Had

Mr. Whitson taught sixth-grade science. On the first day of class, he gave us a lecture about a creature called the cattywampus, an **ill-adapted**(适应性差的) **nocturnal**(夜间活动的) animal that was wiped out during the Ice Age. He passed around a **skull**(颅骨) as he talked. We all took notes and later had a test.

When he returned my paper, I was shocked. There was a big red × through each of my answers. I had failed. There had to be some mistake! I had written down exactly what Mr. Whitson said. Then I realized that everyone in the class had failed. What had happened?

Very simple, Mr. Whitson explained. He had made up **all the stuff**(瞎话) about the cattywampus. There had never been any such animal. The information in our notes was, therefore, incorrect. Did we expect **credit**(学分) for incorrect answers?

Needless to say, we were **outraged**(愤怒). What kind of test was this? And what kind of teacher?

We should have figured it out, Mr. Whitson said. After all, at the every moment he was passing around the cattywampus skull (in truth, a cat's), hadn't he been telling us that no **trace**(痕迹) of the animal remained? He had described its amazing **night vision**(夜视能力), the

26

color of its fur and any number of other facts he couldn't have known. He had given the animal a ridiculous name, and we still hadn't been **suspicious**(怀疑的). The zeroes on our papers would be recorded in his grade book, he said. And they were.

Mr. Whitson said he hoped we would learn something from this experience. Teachers and textbooks are not always right. In fact, no one is. He told us not to let our minds go to sleep, and to speak up if we ever thought he or the textbook was wrong.

Every class was an adventure with Mr. Whitson. I can still remember some science periods almost from beginning to end. One day he told us that his **Volkswagon**(大众牌汽车) was a living **organism** (生物). It took us two full days to put together a **refutation**(驳斥) he would accept. He didn't **let us off the hook**(放开我们) until we had proved not only that we knew what an organism was but also that we had the **fortitude**(勇气) to stand up for the truth.

We carried our brand-new **skepticism**(怀疑态度) into all our classes. This caused problems for the other teachers, who weren't used to being challenged. Our history teacher would be lecturing about something, and then there would be clearings of the throat and someone would say "cattywampus".

If I'm ever asked to propose a solution to the problems in our schools, it will be Mr. Whitson. I haven't made any great scientific discoveries, but Mr. Whitson's class gave me and my classmates something just as important: the courage to look at people in the eye and tell them.

Not everyone sees the value in this. I once told an elementary school teacher about Mr. Whitson. The teacher was **appalled**(惊骇的).

"He shouldn't have fooled you like that," he said.

I looked at that teacher right in the eye and told him, "You are wrong."

11

A Great Mistake

I work as a postal letter carrier in Charlotte. One day a couple of years ago, I drove up to a mailbox. Christy, the young **divorcee**(离了婚的人) who lived there, was waiting by the roadside. She said that she had a story to tell me.

About six months earlier, it seemed that I had delivered a letter to her, which had her street number on it but was addressed to another house with the same number on a different street in the neighborhood. She decided to **drop off**(送到) the letter at the correct house.

It turned out that the letter had been intended for Johnson, who happened to be single. They talked for a little while, and later on he called. Then they started dating and had been going out together ever since.

I was embarrassed about delivering the letter wrong, but I was pleased that I had brought these nice people together.

A few months later, a For Sale sign went up in Christy's yard, and then the wedding invitations were sent out. Soon the house was sold, the wedding happened, and Christy and her kids moved into Johnson's house.

A few months later, I saw a For Sale sign in their yard. I feared the marriage might be in trouble, so I made up an excuse to go to their door and check on them.

Christy opened the door, smiled broadly, and pointed to her huge stomach. "We're having twins!" she said. "This house won't be big enough, so we have to move."

As I walked back to my truck, I was suddenly overwhelmed by the thought that one **misdelivered**(错投的) letter was now giving two little yet-to-be-born people a **shot**(机会) at life. Awesome!

12
You Are My Life

There was a boy who was sent to a **boarding school**(寄宿学校). He used to be the brightest student in his class. He was at the top in every competition. But things changed after that. His grades started dropping. He hated being in a group. He was lonely all the time. He felt worthless and that no one loved him.

His parents began to worry. But even they did not know what was wrong. So his Dad decided to visit the school and talk with him.

They sat on the bank of the lake near the school. The father started asking him **casual**(随便的) questions about his classes, teachers and sports.

Then he asked, "Do you know, son, why I am here today?"

The boy said, "To check my grades?"

"No, no," his Dad replied. "I am here to tell you that you are the most important person for me. I want to see you happy. I don't care about grades. I care about you. I care about your happiness. YOU ARE MY LIFE."

Now the boy had everything he wanted. He knew there was someone on this Earth who cared for him deeply. He meant the world to someone.

Thanks a lot, Dad. YOU ARE MY LIFE.

13

Speak Out Your Love

In a class I teach for adults, I recently did the "unpardonable". I gave the class homework!

The assignment (homework) was to "go to someone you love within the next week and tell them you love them. It has to be someone you have never said those words to before or at least haven't shared those words with for a long time."

Now that doesn't sound like a very tough assignment, until you stop to realize that most of the men were over 35 and were raised in the generation of men that were taught that expressing emotions is not "**macho**"(男子气概的). That is, showing feelings or crying was just not done.

So this was a very threatening assignment for some. At the beginning of our next class, I asked if someone wanted to share what happened when they told someone they loved them.

I fully expected one of the women to volunteer, as was usually the case, but on this evening one of the men raised his hand.

He appeared quite moved and a bit shaken.

As he unfolded out of his chair, he began by saying, "Dennis, I was quite angry with you last week when you gave us this assignment. I didn't feel that I had anyone to say those words to, and besides, who were you to tell me to do something that personal?

"But as I began driving home, my conscience started talking to me. It was telling me that I knew exactly who I needed to say 'I love you' to.

"You see, five years ago, my father and I had a **vicious**(凶恶的) disagreement and really never resolved it since that time.

"We avoided seeing each other unless we absolutely had to at Christmas or other family gatherings. But even then, we hardly spoke to each other.

"So last Tuesday by the time I got home, I had convinced myself I was going to tell my father I loved him. It's **weird**(古怪), but just making that decision seemed to lift a heavy load off my chest.

"When I got home, I rushed into the house to tell my wife what I was going to do. She was already in bed, but I woke her up anyway. When I told her, she didn't just get out of bed, she **catapulted**(弹跳) out and hugged me, and for the first time in our married life she saw me cry. We stayed up half the night drinking coffee and talking. It was great!

"The next morning I was up bright and early. I was so excited I could hardly sleep. I got to the office early and accomplished more work in two hours than I had the whole day before.

"At 9:00 I called my Dad to see if I could come over after work. When he answered the phone, I just said, 'Dad, can I come over after work tonight? I have something to tell you.' My dad responded with a **grumpy**(含怒的) 'Now what?' I assured him it wouldn't take long, so he finally agreed.

"At 5:30, I was at my parents' house ringing the doorbell, praying that Dad would answer the door. I was afraid if Mom answered that I would **chicken out**(退缩) and tell her instead. But as luck would have it, Dad did answer the door.

"I didn't waste any time—I took one step in the door and said, 'Dad, I just came over to tell you that I love you.'

"It was as if a **transformation**(转变) came over my Dad. Before my eyes his face softened, the **wrinkles**(皱纹) seemed to disappear

31

and he began to cry. He reached out and hugged me and said, 'I love you too, son, but I've never been able to say it.'

"It was such a precious moment I didn't want to move. Mom walked by with tears in her eyes. I just waved and blew her a kiss. Dad and I hugged for a moment longer and then I left. I hadn't felt that great in a long time.

"But that's not even my point. Two days after that visit, my Dad, who had heart problems, but didn't tell me, had an attack and ended up in the hospital, unconscious. I don't know if he'll make it.

"So my message to all of you in this is: Don't wait to do the things you know need to be done. What if I had waited to tell my Dad—maybe I will never get the chance again! Take the time to do what you need to do and do it now!"

14

Unconditional Love

The following story took place long ago in Israel. One day when government officials were rebuilding a **barn**(仓房), they found a mouse hole in a corner and used smoke to force the mice inside the hole to come out. A while later they indeed saw mice running out, one after another.

Then, everyone thought that all the mice had escaped. But just as they were about to start to clean up, they saw two mice **squeezing** (挤) out at the exit of the hole. After some **endeavor**(努力), the mice finally got out. The strange thing was that after they came out of the hole, they did not run away immediately. Instead, one chased after the other near the exit of the hole. It seemed that one was trying to bite the tail of the other.

Everyone was puzzled, so they stepped closer to take a look. They realized that one of the mice was blind and could not see anything, and the other one was trying to allow the blind mouse to bite on his tail so he could pull the blind one with him to escape.

After witnessing what happened, everyone was speechless and lost in thought. During meal time, the group of people sat down in a circle and started to chat about what happened to the two mice.

One serious Rome official said, "I think the relationship between those two mice was that of emperor and minister." The others thought for a while and said, "That was why!" Thus the Rome official showed his arrogance **superciliously**(傲慢地).

A smart **Israeli**(以色列人) said, "I think the relationship between those two mice was husband and wife." Again the others thought for a while, and all felt it made sense; so they expressed **assent**(赞同). Therefore, the Israeli showed self-satisfaction.

A Chinese, who was accustomed to the firm tradition of loyalty to parents, said, "I think the relationship between those two mice was that of mother and son." Once again the others thought for a while, and felt this was more reasonable. So they expressed assent yet another time. Therefore, the face of the Chinese showed professional **humility**(谦逊).

At that moment, one pure-minded **Samaritan**(撒马利亚人) resting his chin in his palms, **bewilderedly**(不解地) looked at other people and asked, "Why did those two mice have to have a certain relationship?"

Suddenly, the atmosphere froze. **Stupefied**(目瞪口呆), the group looked back at the Samaritan and remained speechless. The Rome official, the Israeli and the Chinese who had spoken earlier all lowered their heads in shame, and did not dare to respond.

In fact, the true love is not established on benefit, friendship and loyalty or blood relationship. Instead, it is based on no relationship.

15

Wind of Forgiveness

The story goes that two friends were walking through the desert. During some point of the journey they had an argument, and one friend **slapped**(掌击) the other one in the face.

The one who got slapped felt hurt, but without saying anything, wrote in the sand: "Today my best friend slapped me in the face."

They kept on walking until they found an **oasis**(绿洲), where they decided to take a bath. The one who had been slapped got stuck in the **mire**(泥潭) and started drowning, but the friend saved him.

After he recovered from the near drowning, he wrote on a stone: "Today my best friend saved my life."

The friend who had slapped and saved his best friend asked him, "After I hurt you, you wrote in the sand and now you write on a stone. Why?"

The other friend replied, "When someone hurts us, we should write it down in sand where winds of forgiveness can **erase**(抹去) it away. But when someone does something good for us, we must **engrave**(刻) it in stone where no wind can ever erase it."

16

So Much to Learn

It was the last day of final examinations in a large Eastern university. On the steps of one building, a group of engineering seniors **huddled**(聚集在一起), discussing the exam due to begin in a few minutes. On their faces was confidence. This was their last exam—then on to **commencement**(学位授予典礼) and jobs. Some talked of jobs they already had; others of jobs they would get.

With all this assurance of four years of college, they felt ready and able to conquer the world. The approaching exam, they knew, would be a **snap**(轻而易举的事). Besides, the professor had said they could bring any books or notes they wanted, requesting only that they did not talk to each other during the test.

They entered the classroom with smiles. The professor passed out the papers. And smiles broadened as the students noted there were only five essay-type questions. Three hours passed. Then the professor began to collect the papers. The students no longer looked confident. On their faces was a frightened expression.

No one spoke as, papers in hand, the professor faced the class. He surveyed the worried faces before him, then asked, "How many

35

completed all five questions?"

Not a hand was raised.

"How many answered four?"

Still no hands.

"Three? Two?"

The students shifted restlessly in their seats.

"One, then? Certainly somebody finished one."

But the class remained silent. The professor put down the papers. "That is exactly what I expected," he said.

"I just want to impress upon you that, even though you have completed four years of engineering, there are still many things about the subject you don't know. These questions you could not answer are relatively common in everyday practice."

Then, smiling, he added, "You will all pass this course, but remember—even though you are now college graduates, your education has just begun."

The years have **obscured**(使模糊) the name of this professor, but not the lesson he taught.

17

The Real Meaning of Peace

There once was a king who offered a prize to the artist who would paint the best picture of peace. Many artists tried. The king looked at all the pictures. But there were only two he really liked, and he had to choose between them. One picture was of a calm lake. The lake was a perfect mirror for peaceful towering mountains all around it. Overhead was a blue sky with **fluffy**(绒毛状的) white clouds. All who saw this picture thought that it was a perfect picture of peace.

The other picture had mountains, too. But these were **rugged**(凸凹不平的) and bare. Above was an angry sky, from which rain fell and in which lightning played. Down the side of the mountain tumbled a **foaming**(布满泡沫的) waterfall. This did not look peaceful at all.

But when the king looked closely, he saw behind the waterfall a tiny bush growing in a crack in the rock. In the bush a mother bird had built her nest. There, in the midst of the rush of angry water, sat the mother bird, feeding her baby on her nest—in perfect peace.

Which picture do you think won the prize? The king chose the second picture. Do you know why?

"Because," explained the king, "peace does not mean to be in a place where there is no noise, no trouble, or hard work. Peace means to be in the midst of all those things and still be calm in your heart. That is the real meaning of peace."

18

I Will Always Be Around

One fine day, an old couple around the age of 70 walks into a lawyer's office. Apparently, they are there to file a divorce. The lawyer was very puzzled, after having a chat with them, he got their story.

This couple had been quarreling all their 40-over years of marriage. Nothing ever seems to go right.

They hang on because of their children, afraid that it might affect their up-bringing. Now, all their children have already grown up, have their own family. There's nothing else the old couple have to worry about, all they wanted is to lead their own life free from all these years of unhappiness from their marriage, so both agree on a divorce.

The lawyer was having a hard time trying to get the papers done,

because he felt that after 40 years of marriage at the age of 70, he couldn't understand why the old couple would still want a divorce.

While they were signing the papers, the wife told the husband. "I really love you, but I really can't carry on anymore, I'm sorry."

"It's OK, I understand," said the husband. Looking at this, the lawyer suggested a dinner together, just three of them. The wife thought, why not, since they are still going to be friends.

At the dining table, there was a silence of **awkwardness**(尴尬).

The first dish was roasted chicken, immediately, the old man took the **drumstick**(鸡腿) for the old lady. "Take this, it's your favorite."

Looking at this, the lawyer thought maybe there's still a chance, but the wife was **frowning**(皱眉) when she answered. "This is always the problem. You always think so highly of yourself, never thought about how I feel. Don't you know that I hate drumsticks?"

Little did she know that, over the years, the husband has been trying all ways to please her, little did she know that drumsticks was the husband's favorite.

Little did he know that she never thought he understands her at all, little did he know that she hates drumsticks even though all he wants is the best for her.

That night, both of them couldn't sleep, toss and turn, toss and turn. After hours, the old man couldn't take it anymore, he knew that he still loved her, and he couldn't carry on life without her. He wanted her back. He wanted to tell her that he was sorry. He wanted to tell her "I love you."

He picked up the phone, started dialing her number. Ringing never stopped. He never stopped dialing.

On the other side, she was sad. She couldn't understand how come after all these years, he still didn't understand her at all. She loved him a lot, but she just couldn't take it any more. Phone was ringing, she refused to answer, knowing that it was him.

"What's the point of talking now that it's over. I have asked for it and now I want to keep it this way, if not I will lose face," she

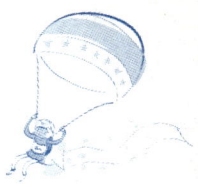

thought.

Phone was still ringing. She decided to pull out the **cord**(电话线). Little did she remember that he had heart problems.

The next day, she received news that he had passed away. She rushed down to his apartment. She saw his body, lying on the couch still holding on to the phone. He had a heart attack when he was still trying to get through her phone line.

As sad as she could be, she had to clear his belongings. When she was looking through the drawers, she saw that **insurance policy**(保险单), dated from the day they got married. The **beneficiary**(受益者) was her. Together in that file there was a note:

"To my dearest wife,

By the time you are reading this, I'm sure I'm no longer around. I bought this policy for you, though the amount is only $100. I hope it will be able to help me continue my promise that I have made when we got married. I might not be around anymore. I want this amount of money to continue taking care of you, just like the way I will if I could have lived longer. I want you to know I will always be around, by your side. I love you."

Tears flowed like river on her face.

19

The Power of Your Actions

One day when I was a freshman in high school, I saw a kid from my class walking home from school. His name was Kyle. It looked like he was carrying all of his books. I thought to myself, "Why would anyone bring home all his books on a Friday? He must really be a **nerd**(傻瓜)." I had quite a weekend planned (parties and a football game

with my friend the following afternoon), so I shrugged my shoulders and went on.

As I was walking, I saw a group of kids running toward him. They ran at him, knocking all his books out of his arms and **tripping**(绊倒) him so he landed in the dirt. His glasses went flying, and I saw them land in the grass about ten feet from him. He looked up and I saw this terrible sadness in his eyes.

My heart went out to him, so I jogged over to him. As he crawled around looking for his glasses, I saw a tear in his eye.

I handed him his glasses and said, "Those guys are **jerks**(混蛋). They really should **get lives**(坐一辈子牢)."

He looked at me and said, "Hey, thanks!" There was a big smile on his face. It was one of those smiles that showed real gratitude. I helped him pick up his books, and asked him where he lived. It turned out he lived near me, so I asked him why I had never seen him before. He said he had gone to private school before coming to this school.

I would have never hung out with a private school kid before. We talked all the way home, and I carried his books. He turned out to be a pretty cool kid. I asked him if he wanted to play football on Saturday with me and my friends. He said yes. We hung all weekend, and the more I got to know Kyle, the more I liked him. And my friends thought the same of him. Monday morning came, and there was Kyle with the huge stack of books again. I stopped him and said, "Damn boy, you are gonna really build some serious muscles with this pile of books every day!" He just laughed and handed me half the books. Over the next four years, Kyle and I became best friends.

When we were seniors, we began to think about college. Kyle decided on Georgetown, and I was going to Duke. I knew that we would always be friends, that the miles would never be a problem. He was going to be a doctor, and I was going for business on a football scholarship. Kyle was **valedictorian**(致告别词者) of our class. He

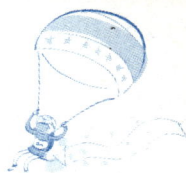

had to prepare a speech for graduation. I was so glad it wasn't me having to get up there and speak.

Graduation day arrived. I saw Kyle and he looked great. He was one of those guys that really found himself during high school. He filled out and actually looked good in glasses. He had more dates than me and all the girls loved him!

Boy, sometimes I was jealous. Today was one of those days. I could see that he was nervous about his speech. So, I **smacked**(拍) him on the back and said, "Hey, big guy, you'll be great!"

He looked at me with one of those looks (the really grateful one) and smiled. "Thanks," he said.

As he started his speech, he cleared his throat, and began: "Graduation is a time to thank those who helped you make it through those tough years. Your parents, your teachers, your **siblings**(兄弟姐妹), maybe a coach…but mostly your friends. I am here to tell all of you that being a friend to someone is the best gift you can give them. I am going to tell you a story."

I stared at my friend in disbelief as he told the story of the first day we met. He had planned to kill himself over the weekend. He talked of how he had cleaned out his **locker**(寄物柜) so his Mom wouldn't have to do it later and was carrying his stuff home. He looked hard at me and gave me a little smile. "Thankfully, I was saved. My friend saved me from doing the unspeakable."

I heard the gasp go through the crowd as this handsome, popular boy told us all about his weakest moment. I saw his Mom and Dad looking at me and smiling that same grateful smile. Not until that moment did I realize its depth.

20

Let Your Love Be Known

There was once a guy who suffered from cancer, a cancer that can't be cured. He was 18 years old and he could die anytime. All his life, he was stuck in his house being taken cared of by his mother. He never went outside but he was sick of staying home and wanted to go out for once. So he asked his mother and she gave him permission.

He walked down his block and found a lot of stores. He passed a CD store and looked through the front door for a second as he walked. He stopped and went back to look into the store. He saw a beautiful girl about his age and he knew it was love at first sight. He opened the door and walked in, not looking at anything else but her. He walked closer and closer until he was finally at the front desk where she sat.

She looked up and asked, "Can I help you?"

She smiled and he thought it was the most beautiful smile he had ever seen before and wanted to kiss her right there.

He said, "Uh...Yeah...Umm...I would like to buy a CD."

He picked one out and gave her the money for it.

"Would you like me to wrap it for you?" she asked, smiling her cute smile again.

He nodded and she went to the back. She came back with the

wrapped CD and gave it to him. He took it and walked out of the store.

From then on, he went to that store every day and bought a CD, and she wrapped it for him. He took the CD home and put it in his closet. He was still too shy to ask her out. He really wanted to, but he couldn't. His mother found out about this and told him to just ask her. So the next day, he took all his courage and went to the store as usual. He bought a CD as he did every day, and once again she went to the back of the store and came back with it wrapped. He took it. When she wasn't looking, he left his phone number on the desk and ran out.

One day the phone rang, the mother picked it up and said, "Hello?"

It was the girl!!! The mother started to cry and said, "You don't know? He passed away yesterday…"

The line was quiet except for the cries of the boy's mother. Later in the day, the mother went into the boy's room because she wanted to remember him. She thought she would start by looking at his clothes. So she opened the closet.

She was face to face with piles and piles and piles of unopened CDs. She was surprised to find all these CDs. She picked one up and started to open it. Inside, there was a CD. As she took it out of the **wrapper**(包装纸), out fell a piece of paper. The mother picked it up and started to read it. It said, "Hi. I think U R really cute. Do U want to go out with me? Love, Jocelyn."

The mother was deeply moved and opened another CD. Again there was a piece of paper. It said, "Hi. I think U R really cute. Do U want to go out with me? Love, Jocelyn."

21

I'll Always Be There for You

In 1989 an 8.2 earthquake almost **flattened**(铲平) America, killing over 30,000 people in less than four minutes. In the midst of utter **devastation**(毁灭) and **chaos**(混乱), a father left his wife safely at home and rushed to the school where his son was supposed to be, only to discover that the building was as flat as a pancake.

After the unforgettably **initial**(最初的) shock, he remembered the promise he had made to his son: "No matter what happens, I'll always be there for you!" And tears began to fill his eyes. As he looked at the pile of **ruins**(废墟) that once was the school, it looked hopeless, but he kept remembering his commitment to his son.

He began to direct his attention towards where he walked his son to class at school each morning. Remembering his son's classroom would be in the back right corner of the building, he rushed there and started digging through the ruins.

As he was digging, other helpless parents arrived, clutching their hearts, saying, "My son!" "My daughter!" Other well-meaning parents tried to pull him off what was left of the school, saying, "It's too late! They're all dead!" "You can't help! Go home!" "Come on,

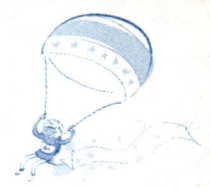

face reality, there's nothing you can do!"

To each parent he responded with one line: "Are you going to help me now?" And then he continued to dig for his son, stone by stone. The police came and tried to pull him off the school's ruins, saying, "Fires are breaking out, **explosions**(爆炸) are happening everywhere. You're in danger. We'll take care of it. Go home." But this loving, caring father still asked, "Are you going to help me now?"

The police went on, "You're angry, anxious and it's over. You're endangering others. Go home. We'll handle it!" To which he replied, "Are you going to help me now?" No one helped.

Courageously he went on alone because he needed to know for himself: "Is my boy alive or is he dead?" He dug for eight hours...12 hours...24 hours...36 hours...then, in the 38th hour, he pulled back a large stone and heard his son's voice. He screamed his son's name, "ARMAND!" He heard back, "Dad!?! It's me, Dad! I told the other kids not to worry. I told them that if you were alive, you'd save me. And when you saved me, they'd be saved. You promised 'No matter what happens, I'll always be there for you!' You did it, Dad!"

"What's going on in there? How is it?" the father asked.

"There are 14 of us left out of 33, Dad. We're scared, hungry, thirsty and thankful you're here. When the building collapsed, it made a **triangle**(三角形), and it saved us."

"Come out, boy!"

"No, Dad! Let the other kids out first, because I know you'll get me! No matter what happens, I know you'll always be there for me!"

22

If I Lose Honesty,
I Won't Be Happy Forever

In the busy city of New York, such an astonishing thing happened. On a Friday night, a poor young artist stood at the gate of the subway station, playing his violin. Though the music was great, people did not have time to enjoy it, for they were quickly going home for the weekend. But in this case, many of them slowed down their paces and put some money into the hat of the young man.

The next day, the young artist came to the gate of the subway station, and put his hat on the ground gracefully. Different from the day before, he took out a large piece of paper, laid it on the ground and put some stones on it. Then he adjusted the violin and began playing. It seemed more pleasant to listen to.

Before long, the young violinist was surrounded with people, who were all attracted by the words on that paper. It said, "Last night, a gentleman named George Sang put an important thing into my hat by mistake. Please come to claim it soon."

Seeing this, it caused a great excitement and people wondered what it could be. After about half an hour, a middle-aged man ran there in a hurry and rushed through the crowd to the violinist. He

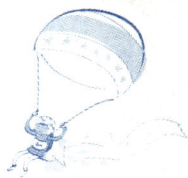

grabbed the young man's shoulders and said, "Yes, it's you. You did come here. I knew that you're an honest man and would certainly come here."

The young violinist asked calmly, "Are you Mr. George Sang?"

The man nodded. The violinist asked, "Did you lose something?"

"**Lottery**(彩票). It's lottery," said the man.

The violinist took out a lottery ticket on which George Sang's name was seen. "Is it?" he asked.

George nodded his head. He seized the lottery ticket and kissed it, then he danced with the violinist.

The story turned out to be this: George Sang is an office clerk. He bought a lottery ticket issued by a bank a few days ago. The awards opened yesterday and he won a prize of $500,000. So he felt very happy after work and felt the music was so wonderful, that he took out 50 dollars and put it in the hat. However the lottery ticket was also thrown in. The violinist was a student at an Arts College and had planned to attend advanced studies in Vienna. He had booked the ticket and would fly that morning. However when he was cleaning up, he found the lottery ticket. Thinking that the owner would return to look for it, he **cancelled**(取消) the flight and came back to where he was given the lottery ticket.

Later someone asked the violinist, "At that time you were in need to pay the **tuition fee**(学费) and you had to play the violin in the subway station every day to make the money. Then why didn't you take the lottery ticket for yourself?"

The violinist said, "Although I don't have much money, I live happily; but if I lose honesty, I won't be happy forever."

23

Dating with a Second Woman

After 21 years of marriage, I discovered a new way of keeping alive the **spark**(火花) of love. I started to go out with another woman. It was really my wife's idea.

"I know that you love her," she said one day, taking me by surprise.

"But I love YOU," I protested.

"I know, but you also love her."

The other woman that my wife wanted me to visit was my mother, who has been a widow for 19 years, but the demands of my work and my three children had made it possible to visit her only **occasionally** (偶尔). That night I called to invite her to go out for dinner and a movie.

"What's wrong, are you well?" she asked.

My mother is the type of woman who **suspects**(猜疑) that a late night call or a surprise invitation is a sign of bad news.

"I thought that it would be pleasant to pass some time with you," I responded. "Just the two of us."

She thought about it for a moment, then said, "I would like that

very much."

That Friday after work, as I drove over to pick her up, I was a bit nervous. When I arrived at her house, I noticed that she, too, seemed to be nervous about our date. She waited in the door with her coat on. She had curled her hair and was wearing the dress that she had worn to celebrate her last **wedding anniversary**(结婚纪念). She smiled from a face that was as **radiant**(容光焕发) as an angel's.

"I told my friends that I was going to go out with my son, and they were impressed," she said, as she got into the car. "They can't wait to hear about our meeting."

We went to a restaurant that, although not elegant, was very nice and cozy. My mother took my arm as if she were the First Lady. After we sat down, I had to read the menu. Her eyes could only read large print. Half way through the entries, I lifted my eyes and saw Mom sitting there staring at me. A **nostalgic**(怀旧的) smile was on her lips.

"It was I who used to have to read the menu when you were small," she said.

"Then it's time that you relax and let me return the favor," I responded.

During the dinner we had an agreeable conversation—nothing extraordinary, but catching up on recent events of each other's life. We talked so much that we missed the movie. As we arrived at her house later, she said, "I'll go out with you again, but only if you let me invite you." I agreed.

"How was your dinner date?" asked my wife when I got home.

"Very nice. Much more so than I could have imagined," I answered.

A few days later my mother died of a massive heart attack. It happened so suddenly that I didn't have a chance to do anything for her. At that moment I understood the importance of saying in time: "I LOVE YOU" and to give our loved ones the time that they deserve. Nothing in life is more important than your family. Give them the time they deserve, because these things cannot be put off till "some other time".

24

A Love Story

A girl and a boy were on a motorcycle, speeding through the night. They loved each other a lot.

Girl: "Slow down a little. I'm **scared**(吓坏的)."
Boy: "No, it's so fun."
Girl: "Please...it's so scary."
Boy: "Then say that you love me."
Girl: "Fine. I love you. Can you slow down now?"
Boy: "Give me a big hug."
The girl gave him a big hug.
Girl: "Now can you slow down?"
Boy: "Can you take off my **helmet**(头盔) and put it on? It's uncomfortable and it's bothering me while I drive."

The next day, there was a story in the newspaper. A motorcycle had crashed into a building because its **brakes**(刹车) were broken. There were two people on the motorcycle, of which one died, and the other had survived...The boy knew that the brakes were broken. He didn't want to let the girl know, because he knew that the girl would have gotten scared. Instead, he was told the last time that she loved him, got a hug from her, put his helmet on her so that she could live, and died himself…

25

A True Gift of Love

In a hospital a woman had just had a baby. She was very happy.

"Can I see my baby?" the happy new mother asked.

When the baby was nestled in her arms, she looked upon his tiny face and gasped. The doctor turned quickly and looked out of the tall hospital window. The baby had been born without ears.

Time proved that the baby's hearing was perfect. It was only his appearance that was **marred**(损坏). When he rushed home from school one day and flung himself into his mother's arms, she sighed, knowing that his life was to be **a succession of**(一连串) heartbreaks.

He **blurted out**(冲口说出) the tragedy. "A boy, a big boy… called me a **freak**(怪物)." She sighed, knowing that his life was to be endless of heartbreaks.

He grew up, handsome for his misfortune. A favorite with his fellow students, he might have been class president, but for that. He developed a gift, a talent for literature and music.

"But you might **mingle**(融入) with other young people," his mother **reproved**(责备) him, but felt a kindness in her heart.

The boy's father had a talk with the family doctor…"Could nothing be done?"

"I believe I could **graft on**(嫁接) a pair of outer ears, if they could be **procured**(得到)," the doctor decided.

Whereupon the search began for a person who would make such a **sacrifice**(牺牲) for a young man.

Two years went by. One day, his father said to the son, "You're going to the hospital, son. Mother and I have someone who will **donate**(捐赠) the ears you need. But it's a secret."

The operation was a brilliant success, and a new person **emerged** (出现). His talents blossomed into genius, and school and college became a series of **triumphs**(成功).

Later he married and entered the **diplomatic service**(外交部门). One day, he asked his father, "Who gave me the ears? Who gave me so much? I could never do enough for him or her."

"I do not believe you could," said the father, "but the agreement was that you are not to know…not yet."

The years kept their profound secret, but the day did come. One of the darkest days that ever pass through the son. He stood with his father over his mother's **casket**(棺材). Slowly, tenderly, the father stretched forth a hand and raised the thick, reddish brown hair to **reveal**(显示) the mother had no outer ears.

"Mother said she was glad she never let her hair be cut," his father whispered gently, " and nobody ever thought mother less beautiful, did they?"

26

The Difference a Teacher Can Make

Steve, a twelve-year-old boy with **alcoholic**(酗酒的) parents, was about to be lost forever, by the U. S. education system. Remarkably, he could read, yet, in spite of his reading skills, Steve was failing. He had been failing since first grade, as he was passed on from grade to grade. Steve was a big boy, looking more like a teenager than a twelve years old, yet, Steve went unnoticed…until Miss White.

Miss White was a smiling, young, beautiful redhead, and Steve was in love! For the first time in his young life, he couldn't take his eyes off his teacher; yet, still he failed. He never did his homework, and he was always in trouble with Miss White. His heart would break under her sharp words, and when he was punished for failing to turn in his homework, he felt just miserable! Still, he did not study.

In the middle of the first semester of school, the entire seventh grade was tested for basic skills. Steve hurried through his tests, and continued to dream of other things, as the day went on. His heart was not in school, but in the woods, where he often escaped alone, trying to shut out the sights, sounds and smells of his alcoholic home. No one checked on him to see if he was safe. No one knew he was gone, because no one was sober enough to care. **Oddly enough**(说来也怪), Steve never missed a day of school.

One day, Miss White's impatient voice broke into his daydreams.

"Steve!!" Startled, he turned to look at her.

"Pay attention!"

Steve locked his gaze on Miss White with **adolescent adoration**(爱慕), as she began to go over the test results for the seventh grade.

"You all did pretty well," she told the class, "except for one boy, and it breaks my heart to tell you this, but..." She hesitated, pinning Steve to his seat with a sharp stare, her eyes searching his face.

"...The smartest boy in the seventh grade is failing my class!"

She just stared at Steve, as the class spun around for a good look. Steve dropped his eyes and carefully examined his fingertips.

After that, it was war!! Steve still wouldn't do his homework. Even as the punishments became more severe, he remained **stubborn**(顽固).

"Just try it! ONE WEEK!" said the teacher, but the boy was unmoved.

"You're smart enough! You'll see a change!" Nothing **fazed**(打乱……的平静) him.

"Give yourself a chance! Don't give up on your life!" Nothing.

"Steve! Please! I care about you!"

Wow! Suddenly, Steve got it! Someone cared about him? Someone, totally unattainable and perfect, CARED ABOUT HIM!

Steve went home from school, thoughtful, that afternoon. Walking into the house, he took one look around. Both parents were **passed out**(烂醉), in various stages of undress, and the **stench**(臭气) was overpowering! He quickly, gathered up his camping **gear**(用具), a jar of **peanut butter**(花生酱), a loaf of bread, a bottle of water, and this time... his schoolbooks. **Grim**(严肃的) faced and determined, he headed for the woods.

The following Monday he arrived at school on time, and he waited for Miss White to enter the classroom. She walked in, all sparkle and smiles! God, she was beautiful! He yearned for her smile to turn on him. It did not.

Miss White immediately gave a quiz on the weekend homework. Steve hurried through the test, and was the first to hand in his paper. With a look of surprise, Miss White took his paper. Obviously puzzled, she began to look it over. Steve walked back to his desk, his heart pounding within his chest. As he sat down, he couldn't **resist**(抑制) another look at the lovely woman.

Miss White's face was in total shock! She glanced up at Steve, then down, then up. Suddenly, her face broke into a radiant smile. The smartest boy in the seventh grade had just passed his first test!

From that moment nothing was the same for Steve. Life at home remained the same, but life still changed. He discovered that not only could he learn, but he was good at it!

He discovered that he could understand and retain knowledge, and that he could translate the things he learned into his own life. Steve began to excel! And he continued this course throughout his school life.

After high-school Steve **enlisted**(参军) in the **Navy**(海军), and he had a successful military career. During that time, he met the love of his life, he raised a family, and he graduated from the college Magna

Cum Laude. During his naval career, he inspired many young people, who without him, might not have believed in themselves. Steve began a second career after the Navy, and he continued to inspire others, as an **adjunct**(助理的) professor in a nearby college. Miss White left a great legacy. She saved one boy, who has changed many lives.

You see, it's simple, really. A change took place within the heart of one boy, all because of one teacher, who cared.

27

A Brother Like That

A friend of mine named Paul received an automobile from his brother as a Christmas present. On Christmas Eve when Paul came out of his office, a street **urchin**(顽童) was walking around the shiny new car, admiring it.

"Is this your car, Mister?" he asked.

Paul nodded. "My brother gave it to me for Christmas."

The boy was **astounded**(惊讶). "You mean your brother gave it to you and it didn't cost you anything? Boy, I wish…" he hesitated.

Of course Paul knew what he was going to wish for. He was going to wish he had a brother like that. But what the lad said **jarred**(使震动) Paul all the way down to his heels.

"I wish," the boy went on, "that I could be a brother like that."

Paul looked at the boy in astonishment, then impulsively he added, "Would you like to take a ride in my automobile?"

"Oh yes, I'd love that."

After a short ride, the boy turned and with his eyes **aglow**(发亮), said, "Mister, would you mind driving in front of my house?"

Paul smiled a little. He thought he knew what the lad wanted. He

55

wanted to show his neighbors that he could ride home in a big automobile. But Paul was wrong again.

"Will you stop where those two steps are?" the boy asked.

He ran up the steps. Then in a little while Paul heard him coming back, but he was not coming fast. He was carrying his little crippled brother. He sat him down on the bottom step, then sort of squeezed up against him and pointed to the car.

"There she is, Buddy, just like I told you upstairs. His brother gave it to him for Christmas and it didn't cost him a cent. And some day I'm going to give you one just like it...then you can see for yourself all the pretty things in the Christmas windows that I've been trying to tell you about."

Paul got out and lifted the lad to the front seat of his car. The shining-eyed older brother climbed in beside him and the three of them began a memorable holiday ride.

28

Family

FAMILY = (F)ather (A)nd (M)other, (I) (L)ove (Y)ou

A man came home from work late, tired and irritated, to find his 5-year-old son waiting for him at the door.

"Daddy, may I ask you a question?"

"Yeah sure, what is it?" replied the man.

"Daddy, how much do you make an hour?"

"That's none of your business. Why do you ask such a thing?" the man said angrily.

"I just want to know. Please tell me, how much do you make an hour?" pleaded the little boy.

"If you must know, I make $20 an hour."

"Oh," the little boy replied, with his head down. Looking up, he said, "Daddy, may I please borrow $10?"

The father was **furious**(狂怒), "If the only reason you asked that is so you can borrow some money to buy a silly toy or some other nonsense, then you march yourself straight to your room and go to bed. Think about why you are being so selfish. I work hard every day for such this childish behavior."

The little boy quietly went to his room and shut the door. The man sat down and started to get even angrier about the little boy's questions. How dare he ask such questions only to get some money? After about an hour or so, the man had calmed down, and started to think: Maybe there was something he really needed to buy with that $10 and he really didn't ask for money very often.

The man went to the door of the little boy's room and opened the door.

"Are you asleep, son?" he asked.

"No, Daddy, I'm awake," replied the boy.

"I've been thinking, maybe I was too hard on you earlier," said the man. "It's been a long day and I took out my **aggravation**(怒火) on you. I'm very sorry. Here's the $10 you asked for."

The little boy sat straight up, smiling. "Oh, thank you, Daddy!" he yelled. Then, reaching under his pillow he pulled out some **crumpled up**(皱巴巴的) bills. The man, seeing that the boy already had money, started to get angry again. The little boy slowly counted out his money, then looked up at his father.

"Why do you want more money if you already have some?" the father grumbled.

"Because I didn't have enough, but now I do," the little boy replied. "Daddy, I have $20 now. Can I buy an hour of your time? Please come home early tomorrow. I would like to have dinner with you."

29

Love Is Just a Thread

Sometimes I really doubt whether there is love between my parents. Every day they are very busy trying to earn money in order to pay the high tuition for my brother and me. They don't act in the romantic ways that I read in books or I see on TV. In their opinion, "I love you" is too **luxurious**(奢侈) for them to say. Sending flowers to each other on Valentine's Day is even more out of the question. Finally my father has a bad temper. When he's very tired from the hard work, it is easy for him to lose his temper.

One day, my mother was **sewing a quilt**(缝被子). I silently sat down beside her and looked at her.

"Mom, I have a question to ask you," I said after a while.

"What?" she replied, still doing her work.

"Is there love between you and Dad?" I asked her in a very low voice.

My mother stopped her work and raised her head with surprise in her eyes. She didn't answer immediately. Then she bowed her head and continued to sew the quilt. I was very worried because I thought I had hurt her. I was in a great embarrassment and I didn't know what I

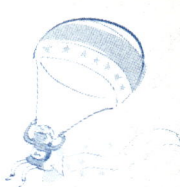

should do. But at last I heard my mother say the following words:

"Susan," she said thoughtfully. "Look at this **thread** (线). Sometimes it appears, but most of it disappears in the quilt. The thread really makes the quilt strong and **durable**(耐用). If life is a quilt, then love should be a thread. It can hardly be seen anywhere or anytime, but it's really there. Love is inside."

I listened carefully but I couldn't understand her until the next spring. At that time, my father suddenly got sick seriously. My mother had to stay with him in the hospital for a month. When they returned from the hospital, they both looked very pale. It seemed both of them had had a serious illness.

After they were back, every day in the morning and dusk, my mother helped my father walk slowly on the country road. My father had never been so gentle. It seemed they were the most **harmonious** (和睦的) couple. Along the country road, there were many beautiful flowers, green grass and trees. The sun gently glistened through the leaves. All of these made up the most beautiful picture in the world.

The doctor had said my father would recover in two months. But after two months he still couldn't walk by himself. All of us were worried about him.

"Susan, don't worry about me," he said gently. "To tell you the truth, I just like walking with your Mom. I like this kind of life." Reading his eyes, I know he loves my mother deeply.

Once I thought love meant flowers, gifts and sweet kisses. But from this experience, I understand that love is just a thread in the quilt of our life. Love is inside, making life strong and warm.

30

A Glass of Milk

One day, a poor boy who was trying to pay his way through school by selling goods from door to door found that he only had one **dime**(10美分硬币)left. He was hungry so he decided to beg for a meal at the next house.

However, he lost his **nerve**(勇气) when a lovely young woman opened the door. Instead of a meal he asked for a drink of water. She thought he looked hungry so she brought him a large glass of milk. He drank it slowly, and then asked, "How much do I owe you?"

"You don't owe me anything," she replied. "Mother has taught me never to accept pay for a kindness."

"Then I thank you from the bottom of my heart," said the boy.

The boy's name was Howard Kelly. As he left that house, he not only felt stronger physically, but it also increased his faith in God and the human race. He was about to give up and quit before this point.

Years later the young woman became critically ill. The local doctors were not able to cure her. They finally sent her to the big city, where specialists can be called in to study her rare disease. Dr.

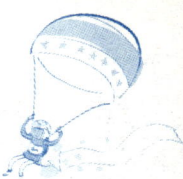

Howard Kelly, now famous, was called in for the **consultation**(专家会诊). When he heard the name of the town she came from, a strange light filled his eyes. Immediately, he rose and went down through the hospital hall into her room.

Dressed in his doctor's gown he went in to see her. He recognized her at once. He went back to the consultation room and determined to do his best to save her life. From that day on, he gave special attention to her case.

After a long struggle, the battle was won. Dr. Kelly asked the business office to pass the final bill to him for approval. He looked at it and then wrote something on the side. The bill was sent to her room. She was afraid to open it because she was positive that it would take the rest of her life to pay it off. Finally she looked, and the note on the side of the bill caught her attention. She read these words:

"Paid in full with a glass of milk."

(Signed) Dr. Howard Kelly

Tears of joy flooded her eyes as she prayed silently, "Thank You, God. Your love has spread through human hearts and hands."

31

Paid in Full

A young man was getting ready to graduate from college. For many months he had admired a beautiful sports car in the showroom of a **dealer**(销售商). Knowing his father could well afford it, he told him that was all he wanted.

As Graduation Day approached, the young man awaited signs that his father had purchased the car. Finally, on the morning of his

graduation, his father called him into his private study. His father told him how proud he was to have such a fine son, and told him how much he loved him. He handed his son a beautiful wrapped gift box. Curious, but somewhat disappointed, the young man opened the box and found a lovely, leather-bound *Bible*, with the young man's name **embossed**(浮雕) in gold.

Angrily, he raised his voice to his father and said, "With all your money you give me a *Bible*?" He then stormed out of the house, leaving the *Bible*.

Many years passed and the young man was very successful in business. He had a beautiful home and a wonderful family, but realizing his father was very old, he thought perhaps he should go to see him. He had not seen him since that graduation day. Before he could make the arrangements, he received a telegram telling him his father had passed away, and willed all of his possessions to his son. He needed to come home immediately and take care of things.

When he arrived at his father's house, sudden sadness and regret filled his heart. He began to search through his father's important papers and saw the still new *Bible*, just as he had left it years ago.

With tears, he opened the *Bible* and began to turn the pages. As he was reading, a car key dropped from the back of the *Bible*. It had a **tag**(收据) with the dealer's name, the same dealer who had the sports car he had desired. On the tag was the date of his graduation, and the words: "**PAID IN FULL**."(全部付清)

32

Hungry for Your Love

It is cold, so bitterly cold, on this dark, winter day in 1942. But it is no different from any other day in this **Nazi concentration camp**(纳粹集中营). I stand shivering in my thin rags, still in disbelief that this nightmare is happening. I am just a young boy. I should be playing with friends; I should be going to school; I should be looking forward to a future, to growing up and marrying, and having a family of my own. But those dreams are for the living, and I am no longer one of them. Instead, I am almost dead, surviving from day to day, from hour to hour, ever since I was taken from my home and brought here with tens of thousands other **Jews**(犹太人). Will I still be alive tomorrow? Will I be taken to the **gas chamber**(毒气室) tonight?

Back and forth I walk next to the **barbed wire fence**(有刺铁丝网), trying to keep my **emaciated**(瘦弱的) body warm. I am hungry, but I have been hungry for longer than I want to remember. I am always hungry. **Edible**(可食用的) food seems like a dream. Each day as more of us disappear, the happy past seems like a mere dream, and I sink deeper and deeper into despair. Suddenly, I notice a young girl walking past on the other side of the barbed wire. She stops and looks

at me with sad eyes, eyes that seem to say that she understands, that she, too, cannot **fathom**(搞懂) why I am here. I want to look away, oddly ashamed for this stranger to see me like this, but I cannot tear my eyes from hers.

Then she reaches into her pocket, and pulls out a red apple. A beautiful, shiny red apple. Oh, how long has it been since I have seen one! She looks **cautiously**(谨慎地) to the left and to the right, and then with a smile of triumph, quickly throws the apple over the fence. I run to pick it up, holding it in my trembling, frozen fingers. In my world of death, this apple is an expression of life, of love. I glance up in time to see the girl disappearing into the distance.

The next day, I cannot help myself. I am drawn at the same time to that spot near the fence. Am I crazy for hoping she will come again? Of course. But in here, I cling to any tiny scrap of hope. She has given me hope and I must hold tightly to it. And again, she comes. And again, she brings me an apple, flinging it over the fence with that same sweet smile.

This time I catch it, and hold it up for her to see. Her eyes twinkle. Does she pity me? Perhaps. I do not care, though. I am just so happy to gaze at her. And for the first time in so long, I feel my heart move with emotion.

For seven months, we meet like this. Sometimes we exchange a few words. Sometimes, just an apple. But she is feeding more than my **belly**(肚子), this angel from heaven. She is feeding my soul. And somehow, I know I am feeding hers as well.

One day, I hear frightening news: we are being shipped to another camp. This could mean the end for me. And it definitely means the end for me and my friend.

The next day when I greet her, my heart is breaking, and I can barely speak as I say what must be said: "Do not bring me an apple tomorrow," I tell her. "I am being sent to another camp. We will never see each other again." Turning before I lose all control, I run away from the fence. I cannot bear to look back. If I did, I know she

would see me standing there, with tears streaming down my face.

Months pass and the nightmare continues. But the memory of this girl **sustains**(支撑) me through the terror, the pain, the hopelessness. Over and over in my mind, I see her face, her kind eyes, I hear her gentle words, I taste those apples.

And then one day, just like that, the **nightmare**(噩梦) is over. The war has ended. Those of us who are still alive are freed. I have lost everything that was precious to me, including my family. But I still have the memory of this girl, a memory I carry in my heart and gives me the will to go on as I move to America to start a new life.

Years pass. It is 1957. I am living in New York City. A friend convinces me to go on a **blind date**(男女初次会面) with a lady friend of his. Reluctantly, I agree. But she is nice, this woman named Roma. And like me, she is an immigrant, so we have at least that in common.

"Where were you during the war?" Roma asks me gently, in that **delicate**(微妙的) way immigrants ask one another questions about those years.

"I was in a concentration camp in Germany," I reply.

Roma gets a far away look in her eyes, as if she is remembering something painful yet sweet.

"What is it?" I ask.

"I am just thinking about something from my past, Herman," Roma explains in a voice suddenly very soft. "You see, when I was a young girl, I lived near a concentration camp. There was a boy there, a prisoner, and for a long while, I used to visit him every day. I remember I used to bring him apples. I would throw the apple over the fence, and he would be so happy."

Roma sighs heavily and continues.

"It is hard to describe how we felt about each other, after all, we were young, and we only exchanged a few words when we could, but I can tell you, there was much love there. I assume he was killed like so many others. But I cannot bear to think that, and so I try to remember him as he was for those months we were given together."

With my heart **pounding**(跳) so loudly I think it will explode. I look directly at Roma and ask, "And did that boy say to you one day, 'Do not bring me an apple tomorrow. I am being sent to another camp?'"

"Why, yes," Roma responds, her voice trembling.

"But, Herman, how on earth could you possibly know that?"

I take her hands in mine and answer, "Because I was that young boy, Roma."

For many moments, there is only silence. We cannot take our eyes from each other, and as the **veils**(面纱) of time lift, we recognize the soul behind the eyes, the dear friend we once loved so much, whom we have never stopped loving, whom we have never stopped remembering.

Finally, I speak, "Look, Roma, I was separated from you once, and I don't ever want to be separated from you again. Now, I am free, and I want to be together with you forever. Dear, will you marry me?"

I see that same twinkle in her eye that I used to see as Roma says, "Yes, I will marry you." We embrace, the embrace we longed to share for so many months, but barbed wire came between us. Now, nothing ever will again.

Almost forty years have passed since that day when I found my Roma again. **Destiny**(命运) brought us together the first time during the war to show me a promise of hope and now it had reunited us to fulfill that promise.

Valentine's Day, 1996 I bring Roma to the Oprah Winfrey Show to honor her on national television. I want to tell her in front of millions of people what I feel in my heart every day:

"Darling, you fed me in the concentration camp when I was hungry. And I am still hungry, for something I will never get enough of: I am only hungry for your love."

33

You Are My Revenge

My grandmother was an iron-willed woman, the feared **matriarch** (女族长) of our New York family back in the 1950s.

When I was five years old, she invited some friends and relatives to her Bronx apartment for a party. Among the guests was a neighborhood **big shot**(大人物) who was doing well in business. His wife was proud of their social status and let everyone at the party know it. They had a little girl about my age who was **spoiled**(宠坏) and very much used to getting her own way.

Grandmother spent a lot of time with the big shot and his family. She considered them the most important members of her social circle and worked hard at **currying their favor**(拍马屁).

At one point during the party, I made my way to the bathroom and closed the door behind me. A minute or two later, the little girl opened the bathroom door and grandly walked in. I was still sitting down.

"Don't you know that little girls aren't supposed to come into the bathroom when a little boy is using it!?" I hollered.

The surprise of my being there, along with the **indignation**(愤慨) I had heaped upon her, **stunned**(使震惊) the little girl. Then she started to cry. She quickly closed the door, ran to the kitchen, and tearfully complained to her parents and my grandmother.

Most of the partygoers had overheard my loud remark and were greatly amused by it. But not grandmother.

She was waiting for me when I left the bathroom. I received the longest, sharpest **tongue-lashing**(训斥) of my young life. Grandmother yelled that I was impolite and rude and that I had insulted that nice little girl. The guests watched and **winced**(畏缩) in absolute silence. So forceful was my grandmother's personality that no one dared stand up for me.

After her **harangue**(训斥) was over and I had been dismissed. The party continued, but the atmosphere was much more **subdued**(沉闷的).

Twenty minutes later, all that changed. Grandmother walked by the bathroom and noticed a **torrent**(洪流) of water streaming out from under the door.

She shrieked twice: first in astonishment, then in rage. She flung open the bathroom door and saw that the **sink**(水池) and **tub**(浴盆) were **plugged up**(堵塞) and that the **faucets**(水龙头) were going at full blast.

Everyone knew who the **culprit**(罪犯) was. The guests quickly formed a protective **barricade**(保卫圈) around me, but Grandmother was so furious that she almost got to me anyway, **flailing**(乱舞) her arms as if trying to swim over the crowd.

Several strong men eventually moved her away and calmed her down, although she **sputtered**(气急败坏地说) and **fumed**(发怒) for quite a while.

My grandfather took me by the hand and sat me on his lap in a chair near the window. He was a kind and gentle man, full of wisdom and patience. Rarely did he raise his voice to anyone, and never did he argue with his wife or **defy**(反抗) her wishes.

He looked at me with much curiosity, not at all angry or upset. "Eric, Tell me," he asked, "why did you do it?"

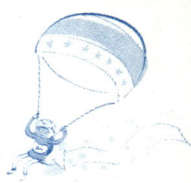

"Well, she yelled at me for nothing," I said **earnestly**(认真地). "Now she's got something to yell about."

Grandfather didn't speak right away. He just sat there, looking at me and smiling.

"Eric," he said at last, "**you are my revenge**(你替我报了仇)."

34

A Gift of Love

In 1945, a 12-year-old boy saw something in a shop window that set his heart racing. But the price—five dollars, was far beyond Reuben Earle's **means**(财力). Five dollars would buy almost a week's **groceries**(食品) for his family.

Reuben couldn't ask his father, Mark Earle, for the money. Everything Mark made was through fishing in Bay Roberts, Newfoundland, Canada. Reuben's mother, Dora, **stretched like elastic**(尽最大努力) to feed and clothe their five children.

Nevertheless, Reuben opened the shop's door and went inside. Standing proud and straight in his flour-sack shirt and washed-out trousers, he told the shopkeeper what he wanted, adding, "But I don't have the money right now. Can you please hold it for me for some time?"

"I'll try," the shopkeeper smiled. "People around here don't usually have that kind of money to spend on things. It should keep for a while."

Reuben respectfully touched his worn cap and walked out into the sunlight with the bay rippling in a freshening wind. There was purpose in his **loping stride**(大步). He would raise the five dollars and not tell anybody.

69

Hearing the sound of hammering from a side street, Reuben had an idea. He ran towards the sound and stopped at a **construction site**(建筑工地). People built their own homes in Bay Roberts, using nails bought in **hessian**(麻布) bags from a local factory. Sometimes the bags were **discarded**(丢弃) in the **flurry**(匆忙) of building, and Reuben knew he could sell them back to the factory for five cents a piece.

That day he found two bags, which he took to the rambling wooden factory and sold to the man in charge of packing nails.

The boy's hand tightly clutched the five-cent pieces as he ran the two kilometers home.

Near his house stood the ancient **barn**(牲口棚) that housed the family's goats and chickens. Reuben found a little **tin can**(锡罐) and dropped his coins inside. Then he climbed into the loft of the barn and hid the tin can beneath a pile of sweet smelling **hay**(干草).

It was dinnertime when Reuben got home. His father sat at the big kitchen table, working on a fishing net. Dora was at the kitchen stove, ready to serve dinner as Reuben took his place at the table.

He looked at his mother and smiled. Sunlight from the window gilded her shoulder-length blonde hair. Slim and beautiful, she was the center of the home, the **glue**(胶) that held it together.

Her **chores**(家务) were never-ending. Sewing clothes for her family on the old Singer **treadle machine**(踏板缝纫机), cooking meals and baking bread, planting and tending a vegetable garden, milking the goats and **scrubbing**(搓洗) soiled clothes on a washboard. But she was happy. Her family and their well-being were her highest **priority**(重点).

Every day after chores and school, Reuben **scoured**(走遍) the town, collecting the hessian bags. On the day the two-room school closed for the summer, no student was more delighted than Reuben. Now he would have more time for his mission.

All summer long, despite chores at home weeding and watering the garden, cutting wood and fetching water, Reuben kept to his secret

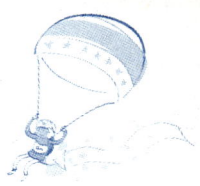

task.

Then all too soon the garden was harvested, the vegetables canned and stored, and the school reopened. Soon the leaves fell and the winds blew cold and gusty from the bay. Reuben wandered the streets, diligently searching for his hessian treasures.

Often he was cold, tired and hungry, but the thought of the object in the shop window sustained him. Sometimes his mother would ask, "Reuben, where were you? We were waiting for you to have dinner."

"Playing, Mum. Sorry."

Dora would look at his face and shake her head.

Finally spring burst into glorious green and Reuben's spirits **erupted**(喷发). The time had come! He ran into the barn, climbed to the hayloft and uncovered the tin can. He poured the coins out and began to count.

Then he counted again. He needed 20 cents more. Could there be any bags left anywhere in town? He had to find four and sell them before the day ended.

Reuben ran down Water Street.

The shadows were lengthening when Reuben arrived at the factory. The bag buyer was about to lock up.

"Mister! Please don't close up yet."

The man turned and saw Reuben, dirty and sweat stained.

"Come back tomorrow, boy."

"Please, Mister. I have to sell the bags now, please." The man heard a **tremor**(颤动) in Reuben's voice and could tell he was close to tears.

"Why do you need this money so badly?"

"It's a secret."

The man took the bags, reached into his pocket and put four coins in Reuben's hand. Reuben murmured a "thank you" and ran home.

Then, **clutching**(紧抓) the tin can, he headed for the shop.

"I have the money," he **solemnly**(郑重地) told the owner.

The man went to the window and **retrieved**(寻回) Reuben's

treasure.

He wiped the dust off and gently wrapped it in brown paper. Then he placed the parcel in Reuben's hands.

Racing home, Reuben burst through the front door. His mother was scrubbing the kitchen stove. "Here, Mum! Here!" Reuben exclaimed as he ran to her side. He placed a small box in her work roughened hand.

She unwrapped it carefully, to save the paper. A blue-velvet(天鹅绒) jewel box appeared. Dora lifted the lid, tears beginning to blur her vision.

In gold lettering on a small, **almond-shaped brooch**(杏仁形胸针) was the word "Mother".

It was Mother's Day, 1946.

Dora had never received such a gift; she had no **finery**(华丽饰物) except her wedding ring. Speechless, she smiled radiantly and gathered her son into her arms.

35

I Didn't Know How to Teach Until I Met You

There is a story of an elementary teacher many years ago. Her name was Mrs. Thompson. And as she stood in front of her 5th grade class on the very first day of school, she told the children a lie. Like most teachers, she looked at her students and said that she loved them all the same. But that was impossible, because there in the front row, **slumped**(弯身坐) in his seat, was a little boy named Teddy.

Mrs. Thompson had watched Teddy the year before and noticed that he didn't play well with the other children, that his clothes were

messy and that he constantly needed a bath. And Teddy could be unpleasant.

At the school where Mrs. Thompson taught, she was required to review each child's past records and she put Teddy's off until last. However, when she reviewed his **file**(档案), she was surprised.

Teddy's first grade teacher wrote, "Teddy is a bright child with a ready laugh. He does his work neatly and has good manners…he is a joy to be around."

His second grade teacher wrote, "Teddy is an excellent student, well-liked by his classmates, but he is troubled because his mother has a **terminal**(晚期的) illness and life at home must be a struggle."

His third grade teacher wrote, "His mother's death has been hard on him. He tries to do his best but his father doesn't show much interest and his home life will soon affect him if some steps aren't taken."

Teddy's fourth grade teacher wrote, "Teddy is **withdrawn**(孤僻的) and doesn't show much interest in school. He doesn't have many friends and sometimes sleeps in class."

By now, Mrs. Thompson realized the problem and she was ashamed of herself. She felt even worse when her students brought her Christmas presents, wrapped in beautiful ribbons and bright paper, except for Teddy's. His present was **clumsily**(笨拙地) wrapped in the heavy, brown paper that he got from a grocery bag. Mrs. Thompson took pains to open it in the middle of the other presents. Some of the children started to laugh when she found a **rhinestone bracelet**(人造钻石手镯) with some of the stones missing and a little bottle that was one quarter full of **perfume**(香水). She **stifled**(遏制) the children's laughter when she exclaimed how pretty the bracelet was, putting it on, and **dabbing**(抹) some of the perfume on her wrist.

Teddy stayed after school that day just long enough to say, "Mrs. Thompson, today you smelled just like my Mom used to."

After the children left, she cried for at least an hour.

On that very day, she quit teaching reading, and writing, and

arithmetic. Instead, she began to teach children.

Mrs. Thompson paid particular attention to Teddy. As she worked with him, his mind seemed to come alive. The more she encouraged him, the faster he responded. By the end of the year, Teddy had become one of the smartest children in the class and, despite her lie that she would love all the children same, Teddy became one of her "teacher's pets".

A year later, she found a note under her door, from Teddy, telling her that she was still the best teacher he ever had in his whole life.

Six years went by before she got another note from Teddy. He then wrote that he had finished high school, second in his class, and she was still the best teacher he ever had in his whole life.

Four years after that, she got another letter, saying that while things had been tough at times, he'd stayed in school, had stuck with it, and would soon graduate from college with the highest of honors. He assured Mrs. Thompson that she was still the best and favorite teacher he ever had in his whole life.

Then four more years passed and yet another letter came. This time he explained that after he got his **bachelor's degree**(学士学位), he decided to go a little further. The letter explained that she was still the best and favorite teacher he ever had. But now his name was a little longer. The letter was signed, Theodore F. Stoller, **M. D**.(医学博士)

The story doesn't end there. You see, there was yet another letter that spring. Teddy said he'd met his girl and was going to be married. He explained that his father had died a couple of years ago and he was wondering if Mrs. Thompson might agree to sit in the place at the wedding that was usually reserved for the mother of the groom.

Of course, Mrs. Thompson did. And guess what? She wore that bracelet, the one with several rhinestones missing. And she made sure she was wearing the perfume that Teddy remembered his mother wearing on their last Christmas together.

They hugged each other, and Teddy whispered in Mrs. Thompson's ear, "Thank you, Mrs. Thompson, for believing in me.

Thank you so much for making me feel important and showing me that I could make a difference."

Mrs. Thompson, with tears in her eyes, whispered back. She said, "Teddy, you have it all wrong. You were the one who taught me that I could make a difference. I didn't know how to teach until I met you."

36

Interview with God

I dreamed I had an interview with God.

"So you would like to interview me?" God asked.

"If you have the time," I said.

God smiled, "My time is **eternity**(永恒). What questions do you have in mind for me?"

"What surprises you most about humankind?"

God answered, "That they get bored with childhood, they rush to grow up, and then long to be children again.

"That they lose their health to make money and then lose their money to restore their health.

"That by thinking anxiously about the future, they forget the present, such that they live in neither the present nor the future.

"That they live as if they will never die, and die as though they had never lived."

God's hand took mine and we were silent for a while. And then I asked, "As a parent, what are some of life's lessons you want your children to learn?"

"To learn they cannot make anyone love them. All they can do is let themselves be loved.

"To learn that it is not good to compare themselves to others.

"To learn to forgive by practicing forgiveness.

"To learn that it only takes a few seconds to open **profound**(深度的) wounds in those they love, and it can take many years to heal them."

"To learn that a rich person is not one who has the most, but is one who needs the least.

"To learn that there are people who love them dearly, but simply have not yet learned how to express or show their feelings.

"To learn that two people can look at the same thing and see it differently.

"To learn that it is not enough that they forgive one another, but they must also forgive themselves."

"Thank you for your time," I said humbly. "Is there anything else you would like your children to know?"

God smiled and said, "Just know that I am here. Always."

37

The Blessed Dress

I got an engagement ring for Christmas. My boyfriend and I had been dating for almost a year and both felt the time was right to join our lives together in holy **matrimony**(婚姻生活).

The month of January was spent planning our perfect Alabama June wedding. My mother, two sisters and I went to Huntsville, the closest town with a selection of bridal shops, to buy the gown that would play the leading role on my special occasion.

We had a wonderful time just being together and sharing silly

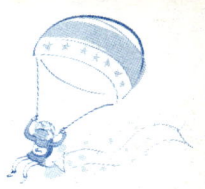

jokes, but the day soon turned serious by afternoon: still no sign of the dress of my dreams. Both sisters were ready to give up and try another day in another town, but I **coerced**(迫使) them into one more **boutique**(时装店).

I had a good feeling as we entered the **quaint**(古色古香的) little shop filled with the scent of fresh flowers. The elderly clerk showed us several beautiful gowns in my size and price range, but none were right. As I opened the door to leave, the desperate shop owner announced she had one more dress in the back that was expensive and not even my size, but perhaps I might want to look at it anyway. When she brought it out, I **squealed**(尖叫) in delight.

This was it!

I rushed to the dressing room and slipped it on. Even though it was at least two sizes too large and more costly than I had **anticipated** (预料), I talked Mom into buying it. The shop was so small that it didn't offer **alterations**(改动), but my excitement assured me I would be able to get it resized in my hometown.

Excitement wasn't enough. On Monday morning, my world **crumbled**(崩溃) when the local sewing shop informed me the dress simply could not be altered because of numerous hand-sewn pearls and **sequins**(金属饰物) on the **bodice**(围腰). I called the boutique for suggestions but only got their answering machine.

A friend gave me the number of a lady across town who worked at home doing alterations. I was desperate and willing to try anything, so I decided to give her a call.

When I arrived at her modest white house on the **outskirts**(郊区) of town, she carefully inspected my dress and asked me to try it on. She put a handful of pins into the shoulders and sides of my gown and told me to pick it up in two days. She was the answer to my prayers.

When the time came to pick it up, however, I grew skeptical. How could I have been so foolish as to just leave a $1,200 wedding dress in the hands of someone I barely knew? What if she made a mess

out of it? I had no idea if she could even sew on a button.

Thank goodness my fears were **all for naught**(虚惊一场). The dress still looked exactly the same, but it now fit as if it had been made especially for me. I thanked the cheerful lady and paid her modest fee.

One small problem solved just in time for a bigger one to emerge. On Valentine's Day, my fiance called.

"Sandy, I've come to the decision that I'm not ready to get married," he announced. "I want to travel and experience life for a few years before settling down."

He apologized for the inconvenience of leaving all the wedding **cancellations**(取消) to me and then quickly left town.

My world turned upside down. I was angry and heartbroken and had no idea how to recover. But days flew into weeks and weeks blended into months. I survived.

One day in the fall of the same year, while standing in line at the supermarket, I heard someone calling my name. I turned around to see the alterations lady. She politely inquired about my wedding, and was shocked to discover it had been called off, but agreed it was probably for the best.

I thanked her again for adjusting my wedding gown, and assured her it was safely bagged and awaiting the day I would wear it down the aisle on the arm of my real "Mister Right." With a sparkle in her eye, she began telling me about her single son, Tim. Even though I wasn't interested in dating again, I let her talk me into meeting him.

I did have my summer wedding after all, only a year later. And I did get to wear the dress of my dreams—standing beside Tim, the man I have shared the last eighteen years of my life with, whom I would never have met without that special wedding gown.

38

Waiting at the Door

My grandmother became a widow in 1970. Shortly after that, we went to the animal shelter to pick out a **puppy**(幼犬) to keep her company. Grandma decided on a little **terrier**(小猎狗) that had a reddish-brown spot above each eye. Because of these spots, the dog was promptly named Penny.

Grandma and Penny quickly became very attached to each other, but that attachment grew much stronger about three years later when Grandma **had a stroke**(中风). Grandma could no longer work, so when she came home from the hospital, she and Penny were **constant**(忠诚的) companions.

After her stroke, it became a real problem for Grandma to let Penny in and out because the door was at the bottom of a flight of stairs. So a **mechanism**(装置) using a rope and **pulley**(滑轮) was installed from the back door to a handle at the top of the stairs. Grandma just had to pull the handle to open and close the door. If the store was out of Penny's favorite dog food, Grandma would make one of us cook Penny browned beef with **diced**(切成丁的) potatoes in it. I can remember **teasing**(取笑) my grandmother that she loved that dog better than she loved her family.

As the years passed, Grandma and Penny became **inseparable**(形影不离). Grandma's old house could be filled to the **brim**(边缘) with people, but if Grandma went to **take her nap**(打盹), Penny walked along beside her and stayed by her side until she awoke. As Penny aged, she could no longer jump up on the bed to lay next to Grandma, so she laid on the **rug**(地毯) beside the bed. If Grandma went into the bathroom, Penny would **hobble**(蹒跚) along beside her, wait outside the door and accompany her back to the bed or chair. Grandma never went anywhere without her faithful companion by her side.

The time came when both my grandmother and Penny's health were failing fast. Penny couldn't get around very well, and Grandma had been hospitalized several times. My uncle and I lived with Grandma, so Penny was never left alone, even when Grandma was in the hospital. During these times, Penny sat at the window looking out for the car bringing Grandma home and would excitedly wait at the door when Grandma came through it. Each homecoming was a grand reunion between the two.

On Christmas Day in 1985, Grandma was again taken to the hospital. Penny, as usual, sat watching out the window for the car bringing Grandma home. Two mornings later when the dog woke up, she couldn't seem to work out the stiffness in her hips as she usually did. The same morning, she began having **seizures**(痉挛). At age fifteen, we knew it was time. My mother and aunt took her to the **veterinarian**(兽医) and stayed with her until the end.

Now the big **dilemma**(困境) was whether to tell Grandma while she was still in the hospital or wait. The decision was made to tell her while she was in the hospital because when we pulled up at the house, the first thing Grandma would look for was her beloved Penny watching out the window and then happily greeting her at the door. Grandma shed some tears but said she knew that it had to be done, so Penny wouldn't suffer.

That night while still in the hospital, Grandma had a massive heart

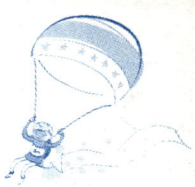

attack. The doctors **frantically**(疯狂地) worked on her but could not revive her. After fifteen years of loving companionship, Grandma and Penny passed away within a few hours of each other. God had it all worked out—Penny was waiting at door when Grandma came home.

39
Love and Time

Once upon a time, there was an island where all the feelings lived: Happiness, Sadness, Knowledge, and all of the others, including Love. One day it was announced to the feelings that the island would sink, so all of them got into their **constructed**(建造好的) boats and left, except for Love.

Love was the only one who stayed. Love wanted to hold out until the last possible moment.

When the island had almost sunk, Love decided to ask for help.

Richness was passing by Love in a grand boat. Love said, "Richness, can you take me with you?"

Richness answered, "No, I can't. There is a lot of gold and silver in my boat. There is no place here for you."

Love decided to ask **Vanity**(虚荣) who was also passing by in a beautiful vessel. "Vanity, please help me!"

"I can't help you, Love. You are all wet and might damage my boat," Vanity answered.

Sadness was close by, so Love asked, "Sadness, let me go with you."

"Oh...Love, I am so sad that I need to be by myself!"

Happiness passed by Love, too, but she was so happy that she did not even hear when Love called her.

81

Suddenly, there was a voice, "Come, Love, I will take you." It was an elder. So blessed and overjoyed, Love even forgot to ask the elder where they were going. When they arrived at dry land, the elder went her own way. Realizing how much was owed the elder, Love asked Knowledge, another elder, "Who Helped me?"

"It was Time," Knowledge answered.

"Time?" asked Love. "But why did Time help me?"

Knowledge smiled with deep wisdom and answered, "Because only Time is capable of understanding how valuable Love is."

40
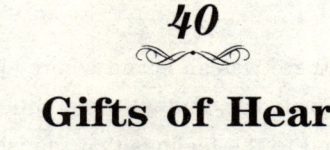
Gifts of Heart

In this **hustle-bustle**(忙忙碌碌) world we live in, it's so much easier to charge something on a credit card rather than give a gift of the heart. And gifts of the heart are especially needed during the holidays.

A few years ago, I began to prepare my children for the fact that Christmas that year was going to be a small one. Their response was, "Yeah sure, Mom, we've heard that before!" I had lost my **credibility** (可靠性) because I had told them the same thing the previous year, while going through a divorce. But then I had gone out and charged every credit card **to the max**(最大限度地). I even found some creative financing techniques to pay for their **stocking stuffers** (塞在儿童袜中的圣诞节礼物). This year was definitely going to be different, but they weren't buying it.

A week before Christmas, I asked myself, "What do I have that will make this Christmas special?" In all the houses that we had lived in before the divorce, I had always found time to do the **interior decoration**(室内装修). I had learned how to wallpaper, to lay

wooden and **ceramic tile**(瓷砖), to sew curtains out of sheets and even more. But in this rental house there was little time for decorating and a lot less money. Plus, I was angry about this ugly place, with its red and orange carpets and **turquoise**(蓝绿色的) and green walls. I refused to put money into it. Inside me, an inner voice of hurt pride shouted, "We're not going to be here that long!"

Nobody else seemed to mind about the house except my daughter Lisa, who had always tried to make her room her special place.

It was time to express my talents. I called my **ex-husband**(前夫) and asked that he buy a specific bedspread for Lisa. Then I bought the sheets to match.

On Christmas Eve, I spent $15 on a gallon of paint. I also bought the prettiest **stationery**(信纸)I'd ever seen. My goal was simple: I'd paint and sew and stay busy until Christmas morning, so I wouldn't have time to feel sorry for myself on such a special family holiday.

That night, I gave each of the children three pieces of stationery with envelopes. At the top of each page were the words, "What I love about my sister Mia," "What I love about my brother Kris," "What I love about my sister Lisa" and "What I love about my brother Erik." The kids were 16, 14, 10 and 8, and it took some convincing on my part to assure them that they could find just one thing they liked about each other. As they wrote in privacy, I went to my bedroom and wrapped their few store-bought gifts.

When I returned to the kitchen, the children had finished their letters to one another. Each name was written on the outside of the envelope. We exchanged hugs and goodnight kisses and they hurried off to bed. Lisa was given special permission to sleep in my bed, with the promise not to peek until Christmas morning.

I got started. In the **wee hours**(凌晨) of Christmas morning, I finished the curtains, painted the walls and stepped back to admire my masterpiece. Wait, why not put rainbows and clouds on the walls to match the sheets? So out came my makeup brushes and sponges, and at 5 a.m. I was finished. Too exhausted to think about being a poor

"broken home," as statistics said, I went to my room and found Lisa **spread-eagled**(四肢展开的) in my bed. I decided I couldn't sleep with arms and legs all over me, so I gently lifted her up and **tiptoed**(轻手轻脚地走) her into her room. As I laid her head on the pillow, she said, "Mommy, is it morning yet?"

"No, sweetie, keep your eyes closed until Santa comes." I awoke that morning with a bright whisper in my ear. "Wow, Mommy, it's beautiful!"

Later, we all got up and sat around the tree and opened the few wrapped presents. Afterward the children were given their three envelopes. We read the words with teary eyes and red noses. Then we got to "the baby of the family's" notes. Erik, at 8, wasn't expecting to hear anything nice.

His brother had written, "What I love about my brother Erik is that he's not afraid of anything."

Mia had written, "What I love about my brother Erik is that he can talk to anybody!"

Lisa had written, "What I love about my brother Erik is that he can climb trees higher than anyone!"

I felt a gentle **tug**(拉) at my sleeve, then a small hand cupped around my ear and Erik whispered, "Gee, Mom, I didn't even know they liked me!"

In the worst of times, creativity and **resourcefulness**(足智多谋) had given us the best of times. I'm now back on my feet financially, and we've had many "big" Christmases with lots of presents under the tree, but when asked which Christmas is our favorite, we all remember that one.

41

True Forgiveness

Forty-three years seems like a long time to remember the name of a mere acquaintance. I have duly forgotten the name of an old lady who was a customer on my **paper route**(送报途中) when I was a twelve-year-old boy in Marinette, Wisconsin back in 1954. Yet it seems like just yesterday that she taught me a lesson in forgiveness that I can only hope to pass on to someone else someday.

On a mindless Saturday afternoon, a friend and I were throwing rocks onto the roof of the old lady's house from a **secluded**(隐蔽的) spot in her backyard. The object of our play was to observe how the rocks changed to **missiles**(导弹) as they rolled to the roof's edge and shot out into the yard like **comets**(彗星) falling from the sky.

I found myself a perfectly smooth rock and sent it for a ride. The stone was too smooth, however, so it slipped from my hand as I let it go and headed straight for a small window on the old lady's back **porch** (门廊). At the sound of broken glass, we took off from the old lady's yard faster than any of our missiles flew off her roof.

I was too scared about getting caught that first night to be concerned about the old lady with the broken porch window.

85

However, a few days later, when I was sure that I hadn't been discovered, I started to feel guilty for her misfortune. She still greeted me with a smile each day when I gave her the paper, but I was no longer able to act comfortably in her presence.

I made up my mind that I would save my paper delivery money, and in three weeks I had the seven dollars that I calculated would cover the cost of her window. I put the money in an envelope with a note explaining that I was sorry for breaking her window and hoped that the seven dollars would cover the cost for repairing it.

I waited until it was dark, walked quietly to the old lady's house, and put the envelope of **retribution**(赔偿) through the letter slot in her door. My soul felt **redeemed**(得到救赎) and I couldn't wait for the freedom of, once again, looking straight into the old lady's eyes.

The next day, I handed the old lady her paper and was able to return the warm smile that I was receiving from her. She thanked me for the paper and said, "Here, I have something for you." It was a bag of cookies. I thanked her and proceeded to eat the cookies as I continued my route.

After several cookies, I felt an envelope and pulled it out of the bag. When I opened the envelope, I was stunned. Inside was the seven dollars and a short note that said, "I'm proud of you."

42

The Little Girl Who Dared to Wish

As Amy Hagadorn rounded the corner across the hall from her classroom, she **collided with**(与……相撞) a tall boy from the fifth grade running in the opposite direction.

"Watch it, **squirt**(小不点)." The boy yelled as he **dodged**(闪

躲) around the little third-grader. Then, with a **smirk**(假笑) on his face, the boy took hold of his right leg and **mimicked**(模仿) the way Amy **limped**(瘸行) when she walked.

Amy closed her eyes. "Ignore him," she told herself as she headed for her classroom.

But at the end of the day, Amy was still thinking about the tall boy's mean teasing. It wasn't as if he were the only one. It seemed that ever since Amy started the third grade, someone teased her every single day. Kids teased her about her speech or her limping. Amy was tired of it. Sometimes, even in a classroom full of other students, the teasing made her feel all alone.

Back home at the dinner table that evening, Amy was quiet. Her mother knew that things were not going well at school. That's why Patti Hagadorn was happy to have some exciting news to share with her daughter.

"There's a Christmas wish contest on the radio station," Amy's Mom announced. "Write a letter to Santa, and you might win a prize. I think someone at this table with blonde curly hair should enter."

Amy **giggled**(咯咯笑). The contest sounded like fun. She started thinking about what she wanted most for Christmas.

A smile took hold of Amy when the idea first came to her. Out came pencil and paper, and Amy went to work on her letter. "Dear Santa Claus," she began.

While Amy worked away at her best printing, the rest of the family tried to guess what she might ask from Santa. Amy's sister, Jamie, and Amy's Mom both thought a three-foot Barbie doll would top Amy's wish list. Amy's Dad guessed a picture book. But Amy wasn't ready to reveal her secret Christmas wish just then. Here is Amy's letter to Santa, just as she wrote it that night:

"Dear Santa Claus,

"My name is Amy. I am nine years old. I have a problem at school. Can you help me, Santa? Kids laugh at me because of the way I walk and run and

talk. I have **cerebral palsy**(大脑性麻痹). I just want one day where no one laughs at me or makes fun of me.

Love,
Amy"

At radio station WJLT in Fort Wayne, Indiana, letter poured in for the Christmas wish contest. The workers had fun reading about all the different presents that boys and girls from across the city wanted for Christmas.

When Amy's letter arrived at the radio station, Manager Lee Tobin read it carefully. He knew cerebral palsy was a muscle disorder that might **confuse**(使困惑) the schoolmates of Amy's who didn't understand her **disability**(残疾). He thought it would be good for the people in Fort Wayne to hear about this special third-grader and her unusual wish. Mr. Tobin called up the local newspaper.

The next day, a picture of Amy and her letter to Santa made the front page of the *News Sentinel*. The story spread quickly. All across the country, newspapers and radio and television stations reported the story of the little girl in Fort Wayne, Indiana, who asked for such a simple yet remarkable Christmas gift—just one day without teasing.

Suddenly the postman was a regular at the Hagadorn house. Envelopes of all sizes addressed to Amy arrived daily from children and adults all across the nation. They came filled with holiday greetings and words of encouragement.

During that unforgettable Christmas season, over two thousand people from all over the world sent Amy letters of friendship and support. Amy and her family read every single one. Some of the writers had disabilities; some had been teased as children. Each writer had a special message for Amy. Through the cards and letters from strangers, Amy **glimpsed**(瞥见) a world full of people who truly cared about each other. She realized that no amount or form of teasing could ever make her feel lonely again.

Many people thanked Amy for being brave enough to speak up.

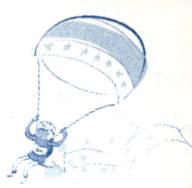

Others encouraged her to ignore teasing and to carry her head high. Lynn, a sixth-grader from Texas, sent this message:

"I would like to be your friend," she wrote, "and if you want to visit me, we could have fun. No one would make fun of us, because if they do, we will not even hear them."

Amy did get her wish of a special day without teasing at South Wayne Elementary School. Additionally, everyone at school got another **bonus**(收获). Teachers and students talked together about how bad teasing can make others feel.

That year the Fort Wayne **mayor**(市长) officially **proclaimed**(宣布) December 21 as Amy Jo Hagadorn Day throughout the city. The mayor explained that by daring to make such a simple wish, Amy taught a universal lesson.

"Everyone," said the mayor, "wants and deserves to be treated with respect, dignity and warmth."

43

Puppies for Sale

A store owner was **tacking**(钉) a sign above his door that read "Puppies for Sale." Signs like that have a way of attracting small children, and sure enough, a little boy appeared under the store owner's sign.

"How much are you going to sell the puppies for?" he asked.

The store owner replied, "Anywhere from $3 to $5."

The little boy reached in his pocket and pulled out some change. "I have $2.37," he said. "Can I please look at them?"

The store owner smiled and whistled and out of the **kennel**(狗窝) came Lady, who ran down the aisle of his store, followed by five tiny

balls of fur. One puppy was **lagging**(落后) considerably behind. Immediately the little boy **singled out**(挑选) the lagging limping puppy and said, "What's wrong with that little dog?"

The store owner explained that the veterinarian had examined the little puppy and had discovered it didn't have a **hip socket**(膝盖骨). It would always limp. It would always be lame. The little boy became excited. "That's the little puppy that I want to buy."

The store owner said, "No, you don't want to buy that little dog. If you really want him, I'll just give him to you."

The little boy got quite upset. He looked straight into the store owner's eyes, pointing his finger and said, "I don't want you to give him to me. That little dog is worth every bit as much as all the other dogs and I'll pay full price. In fact I'll give you $2.37 now, and 50 cents a month until I have him paid for."

The store owner **countered**(反驳), "You really don't want to buy this little dog. He is never going to be able to jump and play with you like the other puppies."

To this, the little boy reached down and rolled up his pant leg to reveal a badly twisted, crippled left leg supported by a big **metal brace**(金属支架). He looked up at the store owner and softly replied, "Well, I don't run so well myself, and the little puppy will need someone who understands!"

44

A Thanksgiving Story

It was the day before Thanksgiving—the first one my three children and I would be spending without their father, who had left several months before. Now the two older children were very sick with the **flu**

(流感), and the eldest had just been **prescribed**(医嘱) bed rest for a week.

It was a cool, gray day outside, and a light rain was falling. I grew wearier as I **scurried**(匆匆走) around, trying to care for each child: **thermometers**(温度计), juice, **diapers**(尿布). And I was fast running out of liquids for the children. But when I checked my purse, all I found was about $2.50—and this was supposed to last me until the end of the month.

That's when I heard the phone ring.

It was the secretary from our former church, and she told me that they had been thinking about us and had something to give us from the **congregation**(教堂会众). I told her that I was going out to pick up some more juice and soup for the children, and I would drop by the church on my way to the market.

I arrived at the church just before lunch. The church secretary met me at the door and handed me a special gift envelope.

"We think of you and the kids often," she said, "and you are in our hearts and prayers. We love you."

When I opened the envelope, I found two **grocery certificates**(购物券) inside. Each was worth $20. I was so touched and moved, I broke down and cried.

"Thank you very much," I said, as we hugged each other. "Please give our love and thanks to the church." Then I drove to a store near our home and purchased some much-needed items for the children.

At the check-out counter I had a little over $14.00 worth of groceries, and I handed the cashier one of the gift certificates. She took it, then turned her back for what seemed like a very long time. I thought something might be wrong. Finally I said, "This gift certificate is a real blessing. Our former church gave it to my family, knowing I'm a single parent trying to **make ends meet**(使收支相抵)."

The cashier then turned around, with tears in her loving eyes, and replied, "Honey, that's wonderful! Do you have a turkey?"

"No. It's okay because my children are sick anyway."

She then asked, "Do you have anything else for Thanksgiving dinner?"

Again I replied, "No."

After handing me the change from the certificate, she looked at my face and said, "Honey, I can't tell you exactly why right now, but I want you to go back into the store and buy a turkey, **cranberry sauce**(小红莓果酱), **pumpkin pie**(南瓜馅饼) or anything else you need for a Thanksgiving dinner."

I was shocked, and humbled to tears. "Are you sure?" I asked.

"Yes! Get whatever you want."

I felt awkward as I went back to do some more shopping, but I selected a fresh turkey, a few **yams**(红薯) and potatoes, and some juices for the children. Then I wheeled the shopping cart up to the same cashier as before. As I placed my groceries on the counter, she looked at me once more with giant tears in her kind eyes and began to speak.

"Now I can tell you. This morning I prayed that I could help someone today, and you walked through my line." She reached under the counter for her purse and took out a $20 bill. She paid for my groceries and then handed me the change. Once more I was moved to tears.

The sweet cashier then said, "I am a Christian. Here is my phone number if you ever need anything." She then took my head in her hands, kissed my cheek and said, "God bless you, honey."

As I walked to my car, I was overwhelmed by this stranger's love and by the realization that God loves my family too, and shows us his love through this stranger's and my church's kind deeds.

The children were supposed to have spent Thanksgiving with their father that year, but because of the flu they were home with me, for a very special Thanksgiving Day. They were feeling better, and we all ate the goodness of the Lord's **bounty**(慷慨)—and our community's love. Our hearts were truly filled with thanks.

45

The Spirit of Santa Doesn't Wear a Red Suit

　　I **slouched**(无精打采地坐) down in the passenger seat of our old **Pontiac**(庞蒂亚汽车) because it was the cool way to sit when one is in the fourth grade. My Dad was driving downtown to shop and I was going along for the ride. At least that's what I had told him—actually I had an important question to ask that had been on my mind for a couple of weeks, and this was the first time I had been able to bring myself into his presence without being **overt**(明显的) about it.

　　"Dad…" I started. And stopped.

　　"Yes?" he said.

　　"Some of the kids at school have been saying something and I know it's not true." I felt my lower lip **quiver**(颤抖) from the effort of trying to hold back the tears I felt threatening the inside corner of my right eye—it was always the one that wanted to cry first.

　　"What is it, Pumpkin?" I knew he was in a good mood when he used this **endearment**(爱称).

　　"The kids say there is no Santa Claus." **Gulp**(哽住). One tear escaped. "They say I'm **dumb**(愚蠢) to believe in Santa anymore, it's only for little kids."

My left eye started with a tear on the inside track. "But I believe what you told me. That Santa is real. He is, isn't he, Dad?"

Up to this point we had been **cruising**(以巡航速度行驶) down Newell Avenue, which in those days was a two-lane road lined with oak trees. At my question, my Dad glanced over at my face and body position. He pulled over to the side of the road and stopped the car. Dad turned off the engine and moved over closer to me, his still-little girl **huddled**(挤) in the corner.

"The kids at school are wrong, Patty. Santa Claus is real."

"I knew it!" I **heaved**(发出) a sigh of relief.

"But there is more I need to tell you about Santa. I think you're old enough to understand what I am going to share with you. Are you ready?"

My Dad had a warm gleam in his eyes and a soft expression on his face. I knew something big was up and I was ready, because I trusted him completely. He would never lie to me.

"Once upon a time there was a real man who traveled the world and gave away presents to deserving children wherever he went. You will find him in many lands with different names, but what he had in his heart was the same in every language. In America we call him Santa Claus. He is the spirit of unconditional love and the desire to share that love by giving presents from the heart. When you get to a certain age, you come to realize that the real Santa Claus is not the guy who comes down your chimney on Christmas Eve. The real life and spirit of this **magical elf**(小精灵) lives forever in your heart, my heart, Mom's heart and in the hearts and minds of all people who believe in the joy that giving to others brings. The real spirit of Santa becomes what you can give rather than what you get. Once you understand this and it becomes a part of you, Christmas becomes even more exciting and more magical because you come to realize the magic comes from you when Santa lives in your heart. Do you understand what I am trying to tell you?"

I was gazing out the front window with all my concentration at a

tree in front of us. I was afraid to look at my Dad—the person who had told me all my life that Santa was a real being. I wanted to believe like I believed last year—that Santa was a big fat elf in a red suit. I did not want to swallow the grow-up pill and see anything different.

"Patty, look at me." My Dad waited. I turned my head and looked at him.

Dad had tears in his eyes, too—tears of joy. His face shone with the light of a thousand **galaxies**(星系) and I saw in his eyes the eyes of Santa Claus. The real Santa Claus. The one who spent time choosing special things I wanted for all the Christmases past since the time I had come to live on this planet. The Santa who ate my carefully decorated cookies and drank the warm milk. The Santa who probably ate the carrot I left for Rudolph. The Santa who—despite his utter lack of mechanical skills—put together bicycles, wagons and other **miscellaneous**(多样的) items during the **wee hours**(凌晨) of Christmas mornings.

I got it. I got the joy, the sharing, the love. My Dad pulled me to him in a warm embrace and just held me for what seemed the longest time. We both cried.

"Now you belong to a special group of people," Dad continued. "You will share in the joy of Christmas from now on, every day of the year, not only on a special day. For now, Santa lives in your heart just like he lives in mine. It is your responsibility to fulfill the spirit of giving as your part of Santa living inside of you. This is one of the most important things that can happen to you in your whole life, because now you know that Santa Claus cannot exist without people like you and me to keep him alive. Do you think you can handle it?"

My heart **swelled**(鼓起) with pride and I'm sure my eyes were shining with excitement. "Of course, Dad. I want him to be in my heart, just like he's in yours. I love you, Daddy. You're the best Santa there ever was in the whole world."

When it comes time in my life to explain the reality of Santa Claus to my children, I pray to the spirit of Christmas that I will be as

eloquent(有口才的) and loving as my Dad was the day I learned that the spirit of Santa Claus doesn't wear a red suit. And I hope they will be as receptive as I was that day. I trust them totally and I think they will.

46
A Guy Named Bill

His name was Bill. He had wild hair, wore a T-shirt with holes in it, blue jeans and no shoes. In the entire time I knew him, I never once saw Bill wear a pair of shoes. Rain, **sleet**(雨夹雪) or snow, Bill was barefooted. This was **literally**(真正地) his wardrobe for his whole four years of college.

He was brilliant and looked like he was always **pondering**(考虑) the **esoteric**(奥秘). He became a Christian while attending college. Across the street from the campus was a church full of well-dressed, middle-class people. They wanted to develop a **ministry**(牧师职位) to the college students, but they were not sure how to go about it.

One day, Bill decided to **worship**(做礼拜) there. He walked into the church, complete with his wild hair, T-shirt, blue jeans and bare feet. The church was completely packed, and the service had already begun. Bill started down the aisle to find a place to sit. By now the people were looking a bit uncomfortable, but no one said anything.

As Bill moved closer and closer to the **pulpit**(讲坛), he realized there were no empty seats. So he **squatted**(蹲) and sat down on the carpet right up front. Although such behavior would have been perfectly acceptable at the college **fellowship**(团体), this was a **scenario**(局面) this particular congregation had never witnessed before! By now, the people seemed **uptight**(紧张的), and the tension

in the air was thickening.

Right about the time Bill took his "seat", a **deacon**(教堂执事) began slowly making his way down the aisle from the back of the **sanctuary**(圣堂). The deacon was in his eighties, had silver gray hair, a three-piece suit and a pocket watch. He was a godly man—very elegant, dignified and courtly. He walked with a cane and, as he neared the boy, church members thought, "You can't blame him for what he's going to do. How can you expect a man of his age and background to understand some college kid on the floor?"

It took a long time for the old man to reach the boy. The church was utterly silent except for the clicking of his cane. You couldn't even hear anyone breathing. All eyes were on the deacon.

But then they saw the elderly man drop his cane on the floor. With great difficulty, he sat down on the floor next to Bill and worshipped with him. Everyone in the congregation choked up with emotion. When the minister gained control, he told the people, "What I am about to **preach**(讲道), you will never remember. What you've just seen, you will never forget."

47

We Are Not Alone

After my husband died suddenly from a heart attack on the tennis court, my world crashed around me. My six children were 10, 9, 8, 6, 3 and 18 months, and I was overwhelmed with the responsibilities of earning a living, caring for the children and just plain **keeping my head above water**(使自己免于负债).

I was fortunate to find a wonderful housekeeper to care for the children during the week, but from Friday nights to Monday mornings, the children and I were alone, and frankly I was uneasy. Every **creak** (嘎吱声) of the house, every unusual noise, any late-night phone call—all filled me with dread. I felt incredibly alone.

One Friday evening I came home from work to find a big beautiful German **shepherd**(牧羊狗) on our doorstep. This wonderful strong animal gave every indication that he intended to enter the house and make it his home. I, however, was **wary**(谨慎的). Where did this obviously well-cared-for dog come from? Was it safe to let the children play with a strange dog? Even though he seemed gentle, he still was powerful and commanded respect. The children **took an instant liking to**(立刻喜欢上了) "German" and begged me to let him in. I agreed to let him sleep in the basement until the next day, when we could inquire around the neighborhood for his owner. That night I slept peacefully for the first time in many weeks.

The following morning we made phone calls and checked lost-and-found ads for German's owner, but with no results. German, meanwhile, made himself part of the family and good-naturedly put up with hugs, wrestling and playing in the yard. Saturday night he was still with us, so again he was allowed to sleep in the basement.

On Sunday I had planned to take the children on a picnic. Since I thought it best to leave German behind in case his owner came by, we drove off without him. When we stopped to get gas at a local station, we were amazed to see German racing to the gas station after us. He not only raced to the car, he leaped onto the **hood**(发动机罩) and put his nose on the windshield, looking directly into my eyes. No way was he going to be left behind. So into the station wagon he jumped and settled down in the back for the ride to the picnic. He stayed again Sunday.

Monday morning I let him out for a run while the children got ready for school. He didn't come back. As evening came and German didn't appear. We were all disappointed. We were convinced that he

had gone home or been found by his owners, and that we would never see him again. We were wrong. The next Friday evening, German was back on our doorstep. Again we took him in, and again he stayed until Monday morning, when our housekeeper arrived.

This pattern repeated itself every weekend for almost 10 months. We grew more and more fond of German and we looked forward to his coming. We stopped thinking about where he belonged—he belonged to us. We took comfort in his strong, warm presence, and we felt safe with him near us. When we saw German come to attention and perk up his ears, and heard that low growl begin deep in his throat, we knew we were protected.

As German became part of the family, he considered it his duty to check every bedroom to be sure each child was **snug**(舒适的) in bed. When he was satisfied that the last person was tucked in, he took up his position by the front door and remained there until the morning.

Each week, between German's visits, I grew a little stronger, a little braver and more able to cope; every weekend I enjoyed his company. Then one Monday morning we patted his head and let him out for what turned out to be the last time.

He never came back. We never saw or heard from German again.

I think of him often. He came when I needed him the most and stayed until I was strong enough to go on alone. Maybe there is a perfectly natural explanation for German's visits to our house—maybe his owner went away on weekends—maybe. I believe German was sent because he was needed, and because no matter how abandoned and alone we feel, somehow, somewhere, someone knows and cares. We are never really alone.

48
An Act of Kindness for a Broken Heart

My husband, Hanoch, and I wrote a book *Acts of Kindness*: *How to Create a Kindness Revolution*, which has generated much interest across America. This story was shared with us by an **anonymous**(匿名的) caller during a radio talk show in Chicago:

"Hi, Mommy, what are you doing?" asked Susie.

"I'm making a **casserole**(砂锅菜) for Mrs. Smith next door," said her mother.

"Why?" asked Susie, who was only six years old.

"Because Mrs. Smith is very sad; she lost her daughter and she has a broken heart. We need to take care of her for a little while."

"Why, Mommy?"

"You see, Susie, when someone is very, very sad, they have trouble doing the little things like making dinner or other chores. Because we're part of a community and Mrs. Smith is our neighbor, we need to do some things to help her. Mrs. Smith won't ever be able to talk with her daughter or hug her or do all those wonderful things that mommies and daughters do together. You are a very smart girl, Susie; maybe you'll think of some way to help take care of Mrs. Smith."

Susie thought seriously about this challenge and how she could do her part in caring for Mrs. Smith. A few minutes later, Susie knocked on her door. After a few moments Mrs. Smith answered the knock with a "Hi, Susie."

Susie noticed that Mrs. Smith didn't have that familiar musical quality about her voice when she greeted someone.

Mrs. Smith also looked as though she might have been crying because her eyes were watery and swollen.

"What can I do for you, Susie?" asked Mrs. Smith.

"My Mommy says that you lost your daughter and you're very, very sad with a broken heart." Susie held her hand out shyly. In it was a **Band-Aid**(创可贴). "This is for your broken heart."

Mrs. Smith gasped, choking back her tears. She knelt down and hugged Susie. Through her tears she said, "Thank you, darling girl, this will help a lot."

Mrs. Smith accepted Susie's act of kindness and took it one step further. She purchased a small key ring with a **plexiglass picture frame**(树脂玻璃镜框)—the ones designed to carry keys and proudly display a family portrait at the same time. Mrs. Smith placed Susie's Band-Aid in the frame to remind herself to heal a little every time she sees it. She wisely knows that healing takes time and support. It has become her symbol for healing, while not forgetting the joy and love she experienced with her daughter.

49

Thelma

Even at the age of 75, Thelma was very **vivacious**(活泼的) and full of life. When her husband passed away, her children suggested that

she move to a "senior living community." A **gregarious**(爱交际的) and life-loving person, Thelma decided to do so.

Shortly after moving in, Thelma became a self-appointed activities director, **coordinating**(协调) all sorts of things for the people in the community to do and quickly became very popular and made many friends.

When Thelma turned 80, her newfound friends showed their appreciation by throwing a surprise birthday party for her. When Thelma entered the dining room for dinner that night, she was greeted by a **standing ovation**(长时间的起立鼓掌) and one of the coordinators led her to the head table. The night was filled with laughter and entertainment, but throughout the evening, Thelma could not take her eyes off a gentleman sitting at the other end of the table.

When the **festivities**(庆祝活动) ended, Thelma quickly rose from her seat and rushed over to the man. "Pardon me," Thelma said. "Please forgive me if I made you feel uncomfortable by staring at you all night. I just couldn't help myself from looking your way. You see, you look just like my fifth husband."

"Your fifth husband!" replied the gentleman. "Forgive me for asking, but how many times have you been married?"

With that, a smile came across Thelma's face as she responded, "Four."

They were married shortly after.

50

All Those Years

My friend Debbie's two daughters were in high school when she experienced severe flu-like **symptoms**(症状). Debbie visited her

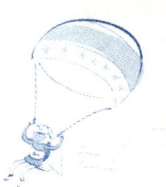

family doctor, who told her the flu **bug**(病菌) had passed her by. Instead, she had been touched by the "love bug" and was now pregnant.

The birth of Tommy, a healthy, beautiful son, was an event for celebration, and as time went by, it seemed as though every day brought another reason to celebrate the gift of Tommy's life. He was sweet, thoughtful, fun-loving and a joy to be around.

One day when Tommy was about five years old, he and Debbie were driving to the neighborhood mall. As is the way with children, out of nowhere, Tommy asked, "Mom, how old were you when I was born?"

"Thirty-six, Tommy. Why?" Debbie asked, wondering what his little mind was **contemplating**(深思).

"What a shame!" Tommy responded.

"What do you mean?" Debbie inquired, more than a little puzzled.

Looking at her with love-filled eyes, Tommy said, "Just think of all those years we didn't know each other."

51

The Smile

I was sure that I was to be killed. I became terribly nervous. I **fumbled**(乱摸) in my pockets to see if there were any cigarettes, which had escaped their search. I found one and because of my shaking hands, I could barely get it to my lips. But I had no matches, they had taken those.

I looked through the bars at my **jailer**(狱卒). He did not make eye contact with me. I called out to him, "Have you got a light?"

He looked at me, shrugged and came over to light my cigarette. As

103

he came close and lit the match, his eyes **inadvertently**(不注意地) locked with mine. At that moment, I smiled. I don't know why I did that. Perhaps it was nervousness, perhaps it was because, when you get very close, one to another, it is very hard not to smile. In any case, I smiled.

In that instant, it was as though a spark jumped across the gap between our two hearts, our two human souls. I know he didn't want to, but my smile leaped through the bars and generated a smile on his lips, too. He lit my cigarette but stayed near, looking at me directly in the eyes and continuing to smile.

I kept smiling at him, now aware of him as a person and not just a jailer. And his looking at me seemed to have a new **dimension**(意味) too.

"Do you have kids?" he asked.

"Yes, here, here." I took out my wallet and nervously fumbled for the pictures of my family. He, too, took out the pictures of his family and began to talk about his plans and hopes for them. My eyes filled with tears.

I said that I feared that I'd never see my family again, never have the chance to see them grow up. Tears came to his eyes, too.

Suddenly, without another word, he unlocked my cell and silently led me out. Out of the jail, quietly and by back routes, out of the town. There, at the edge of town, he released me. And without another word, he turned back toward the town.

My life was saved by a smile.

Yes, the smile—the unaffected, unplanned, natural connection between people.

I really believe that if that part of you and that part of me could recognize each other, we wouldn't be enemies. We couldn't have hate or envy or fear.

52

Miles

One day about eight years ago in the **departure lounge**(候机室) of a flight from New York's LaGuardia Airport to O'Hare in Chicago, I saw a young boy in tears and obvious **emotional distress**(精神痛苦). His mother at his side also appeared upset. Being a parent, I was naturally curious if I could be of assistance.

As it turned out, the flight was full, and they couldn't sit together. The boy was terrified to be separated from his mother. Those were the days when the first-class cabins were not always full and Nancy, the special service representative working with me that afternoon, seated mother and son up in first class.

In the short time we had to chat, we found out that Miles (the boy) and his Mom were returning to their home in Kansas City. They had spent the last two weeks at the Ronald McDonald House at Long Island Jewish Hospital. Miles is a surviving twin (his brother died at birth) and has had serious health problems with **internal organs**(内脏). In spite of his thirty-one major surgical procedures, his long-term **prognosis**(预后) was still in doubt. He would be back through LaGuardia many more times.

105

During his numerous trips, the friendship and bond between Miles's family and the special services staff grew closer, and we'd stop in on Miles during his stays at Ronald McDonald.

Miles particularly enjoyed his flights through LaGuardia as it allowed him to spend time in our VIP lounge, where we have an entire wall filled with autographed pictures of the many **celebrities**(明星) who frequented our office. We soon added Miles's picture to the wall of fame.

Miles's hero, and the person he most admired, was country singer Garth Brooks. Miles would just sit and stare at Garth's picture.

One day, Mr. Brooks was traveling from LaGuardia to Nashville and was relaxing in the lounge waiting for his flight to depart. As he looked at the collection of photographs for any new additions, Garth inquired about the youngster with the big smile. We told him about Miles and the fact that he was currently recuperating from yet another procedure at Ronald McDonald. We also told him how much Miles loved and admired him.

Mr. Brooks left the lounge and headed off to the gate where the rest of his party was waiting.

A few minutes later he was back with his guitar and penned a few words of encouragement inside the guitar case. He asked us to please deliver the guitar and his cowboy hat to Miles at the hospital.

That evening, Nancy and Sam took Garth's guitar and hat to Miles. It was like the gift of life. At first Miles couldn't believe that it was really a gift from his hero. As he comprehended that it was not a dream or a joke, he beamed a wide eternal smile. It was as if any discomfort he was having just disappeared.

On subsequent trips through LaGuardia, Garth would inquire about Miles, and about six months later he asked us to help him contact the family. Garth was going to be performing in Kansas City and he wanted Miles to be his guest. Not only was Miles seated in the front row, but he and Garth also had a lengthy private meeting backstage after the performance.

Although Miles would undergo many more treatments after that special evening, his broad smile greeted us with every subsequent visit, the face of an **ailing**(病的) boy transformed by the joy of a stranger with a guitar.

53

Broken Wing

Some people are just **doomed to**(注定) be failures. That's the way some adults look at troubled kids. Maybe you've heard the saying, "A bird with a broken wing will never fly as high." I'm sure that T. J. Ware was made to feel this way almost every day in school.

By high school, T. J. was the most celebrated troublemaker in his town. Teachers literally cringed when they saw his name posted on their classroom lists for the next semester. He wasn't very talkative, didn't answer questions and got into lots of fights. He had **flunked**(不及格) almost every class by the time he entered his senior year, yet was being passed on each year to a higher grade level. Teachers didn't want to have him again the following year. T. J. was moving on, but definitely not moving up.

I met T. J. for the first time at a weekend leadership **retreat**(集训). All the students at school had been invited to sign up for ACE training, a program designed to have students become more involved in their communities. T. J. was one of 405 students who signed up. When I showed up to lead their first retreat, the community leaders gave me this overview of the attending students:

"We have a total **spectrum**(范围) represented today, from the student body president to T. J. Ware, the boy with the longest arrest record in the history of town." Somehow, I knew that I wasn't the first

107

to hear about T. J. 's darker side as the first words of introduction.

At the start of the retreat, T. J. was literally standing outside the circle of students, against the back wall, with that "go ahead, impress me" look on his face. He didn't readily join the discussion groups, didn't seem to have much to say. But slowly, the interactive games drew him in. The ice really melted when the groups started building a list of positive and negative things that had occurred at school that year. T. J. had some definite thoughts on those situations. The other students in T. J. 's group welcomed his comments. All of a sudden T. J. felt like a part of the group, and before long he was being treated like a leader. He was saying things that made a lot of sense, and everyone was listening. T. J. was a smart guy and he had some great ideas.

The next day, T. J. was very active in all the sessions. By the end of the retreat, he had joined the Homeless Project team. He knew something about poverty, hunger and hopelessness. The other students on the team were impressed with his passionate concern and ideas. They elected T. J. co-chairman of the team. The student council president would be taking his instruction from T. J. Ware.

When T. J. showed up at school on Monday morning, he arrived to a firestorm. A group of teachers were protesting to the school principal about his being elected co-chairman. The very first communitywide service project was to be a giant food drive, organized by the Homeless Project team. These teachers couldn't believe that the principal would allow this **crucial**(关键的) beginning to a prestigious, three-year action plan to stay in the incapable hands of T. J. Ware.

They reminded the principal, "He has an arrest record as long as your arm. He'll probably steal half the food." Mr. Coggshall, the school principal, reminded them that the purpose of the ACE program was to uncover any positive passion that a student had and reinforce its practice until true change can take place. The teachers left the meeting shaking their heads **in disgust**(反感), firmly convinced that failure was **imminent**(将发生).

Two weeks later, T. J. and his friends led a group of 70 students in a drive to collect food. They collected a school record: 2,854 cans of food in just two hours. It was enough to fill the empty shelves in two neighborhood centers, and the food took care of needy families in the area for 75 days. The local newspaper covered the event with a full-page article the next day. That newspaper story was posted on the main bulletin board at school, where everyone could see it. T. J.'s picture was up there for doing something great, for leading a record-setting food drive. Every day he was reminded about what he did. He was being acknowledged as leadership material.

T. J. started showing up at school every day and answered questions from teachers for the first time. He led a second project, collecting 300 blankets and 1,000 pairs of shoes for the homeless shelter. The event he started now yields 9,000 cans of food in one day, taking care of 70 percent of the need for food for one year.

T. J. reminds us that a bird with a broken wing only needs mending. But once it has healed, it can fly higher than the rest. T. J. got a job. He became productive. He is flying quite nicely these days.

54

Playing Cupid

I was lying on the floor of my college dorm room chatting with my younger sister (by a year and a half) about the latest news in our little community while **twirling**(捻弄) the black phone cord around my fingers. Deep in the **mire**(泥潭) of love, she was **gushing**(只顾说) about an all-important upcoming date—she and her boyfriend's first anniversary of dating. She was in a state—would he remember, would

he forget? If he did forget, what did that mean about their relationship? And God help him if he messed this up.

A helpless romantic myself, I filed away this **tidbit**(珍闻) of information, not having the heart to mention that "of course he is going to forget". He was a guy. He might have a general idea of when they started dating, but the **odds**(可能) were good that he didn't have that all-important date **scribbled**(潦草写下) in his diary, surrounded by **intertwining**(纠结的) hearts and other symbols of true love.

I took pity on the poor boy. After all, my sister was **head over heels**(全身心的) in love—the least I could do was give him the small **break**(机会) that was in my power. As was my custom, I headed for home the following Friday, which, as the fates would have it, was the day. Making a last stop on my way out of the college town, I purchased a bouquet of mixed flowers and gently stowed them away for the five-hour drive.

Pulling into the gravel parking lot of our little high school, I headed in to say "hi" to friends and see how my sister's day had **evolved**(进展)—as it turned out, not so well. It seemed as though her significant other had **blown it off completely**(弄糟). No card, no whispered sweet nothings, no acknowledgment. The way I saw it, no surprise, but I knew she was **crushed**(崩溃) and I was all set to **play Cupid**(扮演丘比特的角色).

Leaving my sister, I sought out the **tarnished**(没精打采的) hero. Not in such high spirits himself, he greeted me with a **somber**(忧郁的) expression. Casually, I mentioned that I knew the importance of the day and that I just happened to have a lovely arrangement of flowers sitting unclaimed in my car, and that if he could think of a good use for them, he was more than welcome to **nonchalantly**(若无其事地) remove them from their spot of waiting.

A **lifeline**(救生索) thrown to him, he was off for the car—and I was off to distract my sister. The rest I would learn later that evening as my **re-enchanted**(心醉的) sister told her story over and again for any and all who would listen. He hadn't forgotten! He had merely acted

that way to surprise her. She had talked to me after school, and then he had asked her to go for a ride with him. They had gone up to his parents', and he had a bouquet of absolutely beautiful flowers waiting for her. Could we believe it?! Wasn't it just too perfect?! Didn't we think they were just beautiful?

I nodded, I smiled, I acknowledged her as the luckiest girl in the world, but I'm not sure whose heart was fuller, hers or mine.

One thing puzzled her—she wasn't sure how he had gotten the flowers (the closest flower shop being a half-hour drive from home). She was guessing his mother had made the trip—he wouldn't tell. My little sister was confused, but nonetheless **ecstatic**(狂喜). He had remembered!

Her knight in shining armor had regained his **luster**(光彩), and the day would go down in her diary as a successful step in their relationship.

That was eight years ago. On August 1, my sister and the boy (who, by the way, is a true romantic in his own right) celebrated their third wedding anniversary, and the following day, we all gathered for the celebration of my niece's first birthday.

The part I played in their romance was **miniscule**(微不足道), but it made my sister happy, and that's really the only thing that matters.

55

The Plum Pretty Sister

Justin was a climber. By one and a half years old, he had discovered the purple **plum**(李子) tree in the backyard, and its friendly branches became his favorite **hangout**(常去处).

At first he would climb just a few feet and make himself

111

comfortable in the curve where the trunk met the branches. Soon he was building himself a small **fort**(城堡) in the tree, and dragging his toy tractors and trucks up to their new garage.

One day when he was two years old, Justin was playing in the tree as usual. I turned my back to **prune**(修剪) the rosebush, and he disappeared.

"Justin, where are you?" I called.

His tiny voice called back, "Up here, Mommy, picking all the plums for you!"

I looked up in horror and disbelief. There was Justin on the roof of the house, filling his plastic bucket with the ripe juicy plums from his favorite tree.

When Justin was three, I became pregnant. My husband and I explained to him that we were going to have another baby as a playmate for him.

He was very excited, kissed my tummy and said, "Hello, baby, I'm your big brother, Justin."

From the beginning he was sure he was going to have a little sister, and every day he'd beg to know if she was ready to play yet. When I explained that the baby wasn't arriving until the end of June, he seemed confused.

One day he asked, "When is June, Mommy?"

I realized I needed a better explanation. How could a three-year-old know what "June" meant? Just then, as Justin climbed into the low branches of the plum tree, he gave me the answer I was looking for… his special tree.

"Justin, the baby is going to be born when the plums are ripe. You can keep me posted when that will be, okay?"

I wasn't completely sure if I was on target, but the gardener in me was confident I'd be close enough.

Oh, he was excited! Now Justin had a way to know when his new baby sister would come to play. From that moment on, he checked the old plum tree several times a day and reported his findings to me. Of

course, he was quite concerned in November when all the leaves fell off the tree. By January, with the cold and the rains, he was truly worried whether his baby would be cold and wet like his tree. He whispered to my tummy that the tree was strong and that she (the baby) had to be strong too, and make it through the winter.

By February a few purple leaves began to shoot forth, and his excitement couldn't be contained.

"My tree is growing, Mommy! Pretty soon she'll have baby plums, and then I'll have my baby sister."

March brought the plum's beautiful tiny white flowers, and Justin was overjoyed.

"She's blooming, Mommy!" he chattered, struggling with the word "blooming". He rushed to kiss my tummy and got kicked in the mouth.

"The baby's moving, Mommy, she's blooming, too. I think she wants to come out and see the flowers."

So it went for the next couple of months, as Justin checked every detail of his precious plum tree and reported to me about the flowers turning to tiny beads that would become plums.

The rebirth of his tree gave me ample opportunity to explain the development of the **fetus** (胎 儿) that was growing inside me. Sometimes I think he believed I had actually planted a "baby seed" inside my tummy, because when I drank water he'd say things like, "You're watering our little flower, Mommy!" I'd laugh and once again explain in simple terms the story of the birds and the bees, the plants and the trees.

June finally arrived, and so did the purple plums. At first they were fairly small, but Justin climbed his tree anyway to pick some plums off the branches where the sun shone warmest. He brought them to me to let me know the baby wasn't ripe yet.

I felt ripe! I was ready to pop! When were the plums going to start falling from that darn tree?

Justin would rub my tummy and talk to his baby sister, telling her

she had to wait a little longer because the fruit was not ready to be picked yet. His **forays**(活动) into the plum tree lasted longer each day, as if he was **coaxing**(哄劝) the tree to ripen quickly. He talked to the tree and thanked it for letting him know about this important event in his life. Then one day, it happened. Justin came running into the house, his eyes as big as saucers, with a plastic bucket full to the brim of juicy purple plums.

"Hurry, Mommy, hurry!" he shouted. "She's coming, she's coming! The plums are ripe, the plums are ripe!"

I laughed uncontrollably as Justin stared at my stomach, as if he expected to see his baby sister erupt any moment. That morning I did feel a bit **queasy**(不舒服), and it wasn't because I had a dental appointment.

Before we left the house, Justin went out to hug his plum tree and whisper that today was the day his "plum pretty sister" would arrive. He was certain.

As I sat in the dental chair, the labor pains began, just as Justin had predicted. Our "plum" baby was coming! I called my parents, and my husband rushed me to the hospital. At 6:03 p.m. on June 22, the day that will forever live in family fame as "Plum Pretty Sister Day", our daughter was born. We didn't name her Purple Plum as Justin suggested, but chose another favorite flower, **Heather**(石南花).

At Heather's homecoming, Justin kissed his new playmate and presented her with his plastic bucket, full to the brim with sweet, ripe, purple plums.

"These are for you," he said proudly.

Justin and Heather are now teenagers, and the plum tree has become our bonding symbol. Although we moved from the home that housed Justin's favorite plum tree, the first tree to be planted in our new yard was a purple plum, so that Justin and Heather could know when to expect her special day. Throughout their growing-up years, the children spent countless hours nestled in the branches, counting down the days through the birth of leaves, flowers, buds and fruit.

Our birthday parties are always **festooned**(装饰) with plum branches and baskets brimming with freshly picked purple plums. Because as Mother Nature—and Justin, would have it, for the last fifteen years, the purple plum has ripened exactly on June 22.

56

Daddy's Little Girl

"Will you tell Daddy for me?"

That was the worst part. At seventeen, telling my Mom I was pregnant was hard enough, but telling my Dad was impossible. Daddy had always been a constant source of courage in my life. He had always looked at me with pride, and I had always tried to live my life in a way that would make him proud. Until this. Now it would all be shattered. I would no longer be Daddy's little girl. He would never look at me the same again. I heaved a defeated sigh and leaned against my Mom for comfort.

"I'll have to take you somewhere while I tell your father. Do you understand why?"

"Yes, Mama."

Because he wouldn't be able to look at me, that's why.

I went to spend the evening with the **minister**(牧师) of our church, Brother Lu, who was the only person I felt comfortable with at that time. He **counseled**(劝告) and **consoled**(安慰) me, while Mom went home and called my Dad at work to break the news.

It was all so unreal. At that time, being with someone who didn't judge me was a good thing. We prayed and talked, and I began to accept and understand the road that lay ahead for me. Then I saw the headlights in the window.

Mom had come back to take me home, and I knew Dad would be with her. I was so afraid. I ran out of the living room and into the small bathroom, closing and locking the door. Brother Lu followed and gently reprimanded me.

"Missy, you can't do this. You have to face him sooner or later. He isn't going home without you. Come on."

"Okay, but will you stay with me? I'm scared."

"Of course, Missy. Of course."

I opened the door and slowly followed Brother Lu back to the living room. Mom and Dad still hadn't come in yet. I figured they were sitting in the car, preparing Dad for what to do or say when he saw me. Mom knew how afraid I was. But it wasn't fear that my father would yell at me or be angry with me. I wasn't afraid of him. It was the sadness in his eyes that frightened me. The knowledge that I had been in trouble and pain, and had not come to him for help and support. The realization that I was no longer his little girl.

I heard the footsteps on the sidewalk and the light tap on the wooden door. My lip began to quiver, opening a new floodgate of tears, and I hid behind Brother Lu. Mom walked in first and hugged him, then looked at me with a weak smile. Her eyes were swollen from her own tears, and I was thankful she had not wept in front of me. And then he was there. He didn't even shake Lu's hand, just nodded as he swept by, coming to me and gathering me up into his strong arms, holding me close as he whispered to me, "I love you. I love you, and I will love your baby, too."

He didn't cry. Not my Dad. But I felt him quiver against me. I knew it took all of his control not to cry, and I was proud of him for that. And thankful. When he pulled back and looked at me, there was love and pride in his eyes. Even at that difficult moment.

"I'm sorry, Daddy. I love you so much."

"I know. Let's go home."

And home we went. All of my fear was gone. There would still be pain and trials that I could not even imagine. But I had a strong, loving family that I knew would always be there for me. Most of all, I was still Daddy's little girl, and armed with that knowledge, there wasn't a mountain I couldn't climb or a storm I couldn't **weather**(挨过).

Thank you, Daddy.

57
Is There Really a Prince Charming

A lot of girls grow up thinking that a Prince Charming roams the skies and the plains just waiting for that special moment to come into their lives, snatch them up and carry them away from a world of **shrouded gloom**(满布忧郁的) to one of white, wedded **bliss**(极乐).

When girls flower into womanhood, they are always a bit shocked to discover they are Cinderella or Snow White, and the man they thought was Prince Charming really turned out to be Prince **Clod**(笨蛋).

Marianne had lived a life like Cinderella, sweeping parking lots for a dollar at age eight, trying to provide for herself and her baby brothers as her mother lived daily tackling a mental illness. When she had just passed her teen years, she met the man she thought was her Prince Charming.

She met him where she was a waitress, and he **enthralled**(迷住) her. A musician with a successful band, he seemed to have the widest, most endearing eyes when he saw her. And why not? She looked as sweet as Cinderella, blonde-brown curls, **emerald**(祖母绿) green eyes and a face that echoed of innocence and love, which was really the look of an **awe-struck**(满怀敬畏的) teenager.

All Marianne could think was: He loves me. He loves me. He loves me.

And this was true at the time. With the speed of a **stallion**(种马), the man grabbed her up in his arms and carried her off to marriage. Everything was perfect as far as Marianne was concerned. She had a nice home and enjoyed watching her husband play in his band. She felt loved and adored for the first time in her life. Move over Snow White. Here she comes. And she was about to have a baby.

When her first son, Loren, arrived, Marianne knew something was wrong. He didn't respond to sound. For a year, Marianne struggled and consulted with doctors who told her nothing was wrong.

But finally a specialist announced that Loren was deaf and that there was nothing she could do. She sobbed for the first two years of Loren's life while her husband kept saying that their son was just fine.

Doctors assured them that another child wouldn't suffer such misfortune. But when Lance was born, they soon learned the newborn was deaf, too.

The walls of their already **strained**(紧张的) marriage, which stood on a young girl's fairy-tale dreams, **cracked**(开裂), but they (the walls) **caved in**(塌陷) when Marianne grew angry that her husband didn't want to learn to communicate with his two sons.

He left that to her. She learned **sign language**(手语) as quickly as possible. Her husband wasn't interested. When he talked to the boys, he treated them like they were dogs, patting them on the head, barking out a word or two.

She took her sons to her husband's parents' house. His parents ignored the kids. She took her sons shopping. Clerks gasped when her sons made grunting sounds. And now, she knew about the other women. Sometimes her husband didn't bother to come home. Her friends quit calling her and Marianne felt a biting loneliness.

The stress and the loneliness began to destroy Marianne. She sucked down alcohol like it was water. She fed and clothed her sons, put them to bed, but refused to leave her home.

"Imagine, when your friends and your own family don't bother to want to learn to communicate with your sons," she explained. "You don't have to know sign language. Kindness is a language. We all understand it. When you see a child like this, don't act shocked. Don't gasp and walk away. The message you send to a child is: ' My God, you are a **freak**(怪物). ' You should reach out your hand and smile. "

Smiles, hugs and kisses are what saved Marianne's life. Lance and Loren's eyes were pools of adoration and love—a true love. The type Marianne had never experienced in her life.

It became apparent to Marianne that she could **squander**(浪费) her own life away with alcohol and panic attacks, but she couldn't waste her sons' lives like this. She buckled down and went back to school to earn a high school degree. She got a job with an insurance firm and saved her pennies.

The better she felt about herself, the prouder she grew of Loren and Lance. She started bringing them to visit with her coworkers, who showered them with kindness. It was time for her and her boys to leave their house, cut ties with the father and move on with their lives.

One day, her sons came with her to work, and when she walked into the office of the insurance manager, a man named Eric, she found Loren sitting on his **lap**(大腿). Eric looked up at her, and the skies began to **tumble**(翻滚). He said these simple words, "I feel like an idiot. I'd love to talk with your son. Do you know where I could go to learn sign language?"

Marianne thought she would faint. Not a soul had ever asked her before if they could learn to communicate with her sons. She was shaking inside as she explained to Eric that if he was really interested, she knew where he could learn. It seemed better not to believe him, but he showed quickly he wasn't kidding when he enrolled in the class and began to sign words of hello to her in a few days.

When the kids came in, he took them for walks along the **pier**(码头) near their office. Often she went along and watched Eric, who was becoming a master of sign language, talk and laugh with her boys as no one else had before.

And each time her sons saw Eric, they brightened like the sun and stars in the sky. She had never seen them so happy. Her heart **twitched**(颤动) as though it were being strummed. She began to fall in love.

She didn't know if Eric felt the same until they left work together one evening and took a stroll out on a pier above the Pacific Ocean. He signed to her that he was in love and wanted to marry. Marianne's heart danced with joy.

The couple moved into a small town and opened up a thriving insurance business. They had two more children, Casey and Katie, neither of whom were born deaf, but both learned sign language before the age of five.

And at the happiest moments of her life, Marianne would wake up in the middle of the night, her ear burning in pain, and begin to sob. Her behavior was **inexplicable**(费解的) because she couldn't think of a time when she felt more loved or happy.

Eric would run his hands across her hair, hold her chin and ask her what was wrong. All she could say was, "I don't know. I don't know."

He held her for a long while. Weeks went by and Marianne continued to wake up sobbing. Then, like a **lightning bolt**(闪电), she woke up knowing the answer.

She cried to Eric, her "knight in shining armor", that she wasn't doing enough to help deaf children in the world. She was supposed to help them find their place in society. She was supposed to teach the world how to communicate with these children.

Eric wrapped his arms around her and said, "Let's do it."

Together they formed Hands Across America—"It Starts with You"—an organization that encourages the public to learn sign language and has started making educational videos that use both deaf and hearing children together.

So if you ever have a chance to talk with Marianne and ask her if there is any truth to fairy tales like Cinderella and Snow White, she'll probably say she's learned a lot about such stories in her lifetime.

She's likely to say, "There sure are a lot of Prince Clods out there. But there sure are some Prince Charmings, and there are really a lot of Cinderellas, too."

58

Scarecrow

"Hey, 'Bones'," my brother, Parker, asked me, "what are you going to be for **Halloween**(万圣节)?"

The elementary school party started at 7:00 p.m. The winner of the prize for the most original **costume**(戏装,演出服) got two free tickets for the Sunday **matinee**(日场演出). Parker was dressed and ready to go. I watched him parade in front of the mirror in his **pirate** (海盗) costume. He's so handsome, I thought. All the girls in the fifth and sixth grades were madly in love with him. I'd spent the afternoon defending myself from his rubber sword.

"I'm not going!" I replied.

"Why not?"

"No costume."

"That's dumb," he said. "You hardly need a costume. You're already a perfect **scarecrow**(稻草人)!"

I was used to these observations. Furthermore, he spoke the truth. At twelve, I was already six feet tall and weighed eighty-nine pounds. **Tack on**(加上) red hair and **freckles**(雀斑) and it added up to one thing: I was a scarecrow. School days were charged with **searing taunts**(伤人的嘲弄). "Down in front." "How's the weather up there?" "Are those skis or shoes?" It was hard to smile back, and even harder to make friends.

I tried **plastering**(粘贴) my hair down flat on the top of my head

121

and **prying**(撬) the heels off my shoes. I took **scalding hot**(滚烫的) baths, hoping I'd shrink. In bed at night, I put my feet against the footboard, hands against the headboard and pushed, hoping to press myself back together. Nothing worked. So I saved **nickels**(五分币) and dimes in a **cider jug**(果汁罐) to pay the future surgeon who would find fame in "Ripley's Believe It or Not" by cutting six inches of bone from the legs of the tallest girl in the world and making her the same height as everybody else.

"When I grow up," I told Parker, as he **brandished**(挥舞) his sword in front of the mirror, "I'm going to live on an island where there's no one to stare."

My brother raised his eye patch and looked at me hard. "Sounds awful," he said, and left for the party.

Alone, I listened to the cheerless night and pictured the costumes my classmates had bought. I had tried on a few, too, but nothing fit. I could picture my classmates in their costumes, having a wonderful time. As I wandered about the house, I remembered happier days—before Mommy and Daddy were separated. When Daddy lived with us, he always made me feel loved and wanted. Seeing him now for short visits wasn't the same. The more I **brooded**(沉思), the more my self-pity grew.

Then I saw a **broomstick**(扫帚柄) standing in the kitchen corner. Maybe I could make a costume, I thought. Outside, a sheet and **pillowcase**(枕套) **billowed**(翻腾) on the clothesline. I could be a **witch**(女巫) or a ghost. Then my gaze fell on the back of the cellar door. My father's old **plaid**(格子花呢) work shirt, faded overalls, jacket and cap were hanging right where he had left them.

"I could be a **hobo**(流浪者)," I murmured as I buried my face in the dusty clothes. But Parker's taunt kept coming back at me. "You're a scarecrow."

As much as I hated to admit it, he was right. Well then, a scarecrow was what I'd be. When my costume was ready, I went to school. The closer I got to the school, the louder the cheers and

clapping became, and the more my fears grew. What if they laughed at me? Worse still, what if they didn't do anything? Hiding behind the tool shed next to the gym, I pulled everything out of the pillowcase and started to dress.

Because I was so tall, I could see through the high window and find everybody taking turns on the stage in quest of the coveted prize. Ghosts, princesses, monsters, cowboys, soldiers and brides—they were all there, clad in store-bought costumes, **fragile**(易碎的) dreams for one night. My teeth were chattering. Would they clap for me? Would they whistle and cheer? My stomach ached from **anticipation** (期待).

I'll run home! I decided. No one would know I had been there. But Parker came on stage and glanced at the window. It was too late. He had seen me. If I left now, he'd call me chicken. I watched him bow to the audience and listened to the **squeals**(尖叫) from the girls as he leaped on chairs and tables and **parried**(闪击) with his sword. Next, a small **gorilla**(大猩猩) climbed on top of a ladder and ate a banana. Lincoln gave a brief address. Cleopatra danced with a rubber snake in her hands, and a soldier marched and twirled his gun. Only **Tarzan**(人猿泰山) remained.

Walking carefully through the entrance, I went in, held my breath and prayed, "Please, God, don't let me make a fool of myself." The applause was so loud for the King of the jungle when he gave his call and swung on a curtain rope that no one seemed to notice me walk slowly to the center of the stage. A pillowcase covered my head. With arms outstretched and hands clutching the broomstick inserted through the sleeves of an old plaid shirt, I wore a felt hat and faded overalls stuffed with straw. The room was suddenly still.

Nobody clapped. Nobody cheered. The only sound I heard was the hammering of my own heart. I'm going to die, I thought, right here in front of everybody. The world was tilting, and my ears were ringing when the **hood**(头巾) slid down my nose, just enough so I could peer through the eyeholes. And that's when I saw my classmates for the first

time, as they really were. **Petite**(娇小的) blonde fairies with golden **wands**(棍)—and steel braces on their teeth. A baseball hero with a bat and **mitt**(棒球手套)—and bottle-thick eyeglasses. A boxer with fighting gloves—sitting in a wheelchair.

Someone asked, "Hey, who is that?"

"Parker's sister!"

They looked at one another, surprise brightening their faces. Clapping and cheering filled the room.

The principal came up on stage. "The first prize for the most original costume goes to…"

I never heard my name, only Parker, fear in his voice, saying, "I'll hold those tickets for her. She can't let go of that broomstick or her shirt will fall off."

Later, classmates came over to talk with me.

"How'd you ever get such a good idea?"

"Parker," I said.

"Where did you get the costume?"

"My Daddy."

And in that single moment, I recaptured a memory that had almost slipped away. I was sitting on Daddy's lap and I heard him say, "I love you, sweetheart, just the way God made you." I felt his fingers riffling my hair, and I smiled inside, glad that God had made me a scarecrow.

I left the party early, but not before Nancy had said, "You'll come over to my house sometime, won't you?" and Elaine had **confided**(吐露秘密), "**I get goose bumps**(起鸡皮疙瘩) every time Mr. Allen is our substitute teacher. Don't you?"

I didn't want to stay and dance—the boys' heads came only to the middle of my chest. But on my way home, I decided that Parker was right. A deserted island would be pretty awful. I waited up for Parker that night. I wanted to hear about the fun I'd missed.

"Did you dance a lot?" I asked.

"Sort of," he said. "If you think it's any fun for a fifth-grade guy to dance with a bunch of **puny**(小的) third and fourth-graders!" He

124

kicked at the fringe on the rug and started up the stairs.

"Oh, I almost forgot," he said again. "Here are your two tickets."

"Thanks."

"It's going to be a double feature. One's The Wizard of Oz. Ray Bolger plays a scarecrow." He had reached the fourth step. We stood eye to eye.

"And the other's The Sea Hawk," I said. "Can you believe it? Errol Flynn plays a pirate!"

"Are you taking anyone special?" Parker asked.

"Yes," I said. "Want to go with me?"

59

Love Letters

This past Christmas season, my husband, two daughters and I traveled to Spencer, West Virginia, to visit my parents. During this visit, I decided to explore their **attic**(阁楼). They have lived in their home in the mountains since 1953, so investigating the attic was a trip down memory lane for me.

I pulled down the folding steps and climbed the unstable ladder to the dusty, cold, wood-planked third floor. I looked around and noticed a very old, barrel-shaped covered basket in the corner. I seemed to remember that this basket was filled with old letters my parents wrote to each other during World War II. I opened the lid of the basket, and there they were, letters piled high, faded and dirty—untouched since the day they'd been **tossed**(扔) there.

It seemed a shame to leave them that way. Deciding to read and organize them by day and month, I asked Mother and Daddy if I could take the letters back to my Illinois home. They agreed, and soon after returning, I started my little project. As I opened each letter, all of them delicate with age, I discovered a new and previously unrevealed page in this private chapter of my parents' lives.

My father served in the Army as a **first lieutenant**(中尉), 117th **Infantry**(步兵) in the 30th **Division**(师). His letters were full of frontline accounts of landing on Omaha Beach, and they continued all the way through the Battle of the Bulge. He wrote about his daily experiences with **civilians**(平民), German **POWs**(战俘), **refugees**(难民), **foxholes**(散兵坑), helmet baths and more. I was drawn to these letters like a **magnet**(磁铁). Each of my mother's letters was sealed with her 1944 **magenta**(洋红色的) lipstick kiss. Daddy wrote that he sealed his return letters by rekissing her lipstick kiss. I thought to myself, "Oh, how they missed each other! These letters filled a **void**(空白) in their lonely, war-torn lives."

I finished reading six months of the letters and discovered there were at least eleven months missing. Where could they be? My mother couldn't remember—perhaps, she said, they had been left in her childhood home; she had lived there with her mother while Daddy was overseas. If so, that meant they were lost forever.

Just six weeks after our Christmas visit, Daddy became very ill and was hospitalized. This time, he was fighting a different kind of war. A new **prescription**(处方) for **arthritis**(关节炎) had been introduced to his system, and it had almost killed him. He was scheduled for **kidney dialysis**(透析) when I decided to fly down to West Virginia to visit him. As I sat by his bedside, we discussed the letters. He told me how much receiving those lipstick-kissed letters had meant to him when he had been so far from home.

As I left, the thought raced through my mind that tomorrow was Valentine's Day. But I quickly dismissed this thought. My father wasn't in any kind of shape to shop for a valentine. My parents had been married for fifty-six years. My mother would understand that her valentine would just have to be skipped this year.

Later that evening, Mother and I revisited the attic in search of the lost letters. "Perhaps they are in my old college trunk," my mother said as she quickly located the keys. She unlocked the large sixty-year-old trunk. Lying on top were old tattered clothes from years gone by. We started digging, and toward the bottom, we discovered an unmarked gold cardboard box. Mother said she had no clue what was inside. We both held our breath as I slowly lifted off the top. Yes! Here were the long-lost letters! They were all separated by month, tightly bundled in aged cotton **twine**(绳子).

We took the letters downstairs, and I began looking through them. Lying separate, on top of the bundled letters, was a large envelope. I opened it up. It was the valentine card my father had sent Mother in 1944!

The next day, Mother and I visited Daddy in the hospital. At his bedside, I joked with him, saying softly, "Today is Valentine's Day, and I know you have been a little busy lately, but I've got you covered."

His curiosity was further aroused when I handed him the old envelope. He carefully opened the card, and when he recognized it, his eyes filled with tears.

There was nothing lacking that Valentine's Day after all. My father, in a voice quavering with emotion, read the loving message he'd sent to my mother fifty-six years earlier. And this time, he could read it to her in person.

60

There Are No Vans

I remember one Thanksgiving when our family had no money and no food, and someone came knocking on our door. A man was standing there with a huge box of food, a giant turkey and even some pans to cook it in. I couldn't believe it. My dad demanded, "Who are you? Where are you from?"

The stranger announced, "I'm here because a friend of yours knows you're in need and that you wouldn't accept direct help, so I've brought this for you. Have a great Thanksgiving."

My father said, "No, no, we can't accept this."

The stranger replied, "You don't have a choice." He closed the door and left.

Obviously that experience had a profound impact on my life. I promised myself that someday I would do well enough financially so that I could do the same thing for other people.

By the time I was eighteen I had created my Thanksgiving **ritual** (规矩). I like to do things **spontaneously**(自发地), so I would go out shopping and buy enough food for one or two families. Then I would dress like a **delivery boy**(邮递员), go to the poorest neighborhood

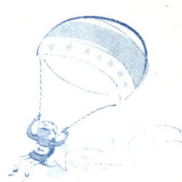

and just knock on a door. I always included a note that explained my Thanksgiving experience as a kid. The note concluded, "All that I ask in return is that you take good enough care of yourself so that someday you can do the same thing for someone else." I have received more from this annual ritual than I have from any amount of money I've ever earned.

Several years ago I was in New York City with my new wife during Thanksgiving. She was sad because we were not with our family. Normally she would be home decorating the house for Thanksgiving, but we were stuck here in a hotel room.

I said, "Honey, look, why don't we decorate some lives today instead of the house?"

When I told her what I always do on Thanksgiving, she got excited. I said, "Let's go someplace where we can really appreciate who we are, what we are capable of and what we can really give. Let's go to Harlem!"

She and several of my business partners who were with us weren't really **enthusiastic**(热心) about the idea. I urged them: "Come on, let's go to Harlem and feed some people in need. We won't be the people who are giving it because that would be insulting. We'll just be the delivery people. We'll go buy enough food for six or seven families for thirty days. We've got enough. Let's just go do it! That's what Thanksgiving really is: Giving good thanks, not eating turkey. C'mon. Let's go do it!"

Because I had to do a radio interview first, I asked my partners to get us started by getting a **van**(货车). When I returned from the interview, they said, "We just can't do it. There are no vans in all of New York. The rent-a-car places are all out of vans. They're just not available."

I said, "Look, the bottom line is that if we want something, we can make it happen! All we have to do is take action. There are plenty of vans here in New York City. We just don't have one. Let's go get

129

one."

They insisted, "We've called everywhere. There aren't any."

I said, "Look down at the street. Look down there. Do you see all those vans?" They said, "Yeah, we see them."

"Let's go get one," I said.

First I tried walking out in front of vans as they were driving down the street. I learned something about New York drivers that day: They don't stop; they speed up. Then we tried waiting by the light. We'd go over and knock on the window and the driver would roll it down, looking at us kind of **leery**(猜疑的), and I'd say, "Hi. Since today is Thanksgiving, we'd like to know if you would be willing to drive us to Harlem so we can feed some people."

Every time the driver would look away quickly, furiously roll up the window and pull away without saying anything.

Eventually we got better at asking. We'd knock on the window, they'd roll it down and we'd say, "Today is Thanksgiving. We'd like to help some **underprivileged**(穷的) people, and we're curious if you'd be willing to drive us to an underprivileged area that we have in mind here in New York City."

That seemed slightly more effective but still didn't work. Then we started offering people $100 to drive us. That got us even closer, but when we told them to take us to Harlem, they said no and drove off.

We had talked to about two dozen people who all said no. My partners were ready to give up on the project, but I said, "It's the law of averages: Somebody is going to say yes."

Sure enough, the perfect van drove up. It was perfect because it was extra big and would **accommodate**(容纳) all of us. We went up, knocked on the window and we asked the driver, "Could you take us to a disadvantaged area? We'll pay you a hundred dollars."

The driver said, "You don't have to pay me. I'd be happy to take you. In fact, I'll take you to some of the most difficult spots in the whole city."

Then he reached over on the seat and grabbed his hat. As he put it on, I noticed that it said, "**Salvation Army**"(救世军). The man's name was Captain John Rondon and he was the head of the Salvation Army in the South Bronx.

We climbed into the van in absolute **ecstasy**(狂喜). He said, "I'll take you to places you never even thought of going. But tell me something. Why do you people want to do this?"

I told him my story and that I wanted to show gratitude for all that I had by giving something back.

Captain Rondon took us into parts of the South Bronx that make Harlem look like Beverly Hills. When we arrived, we went into a store where we bought a lot of food and some baskets. We packed enough for seven families for thirty days. Then we went out to start feeding people. We went to buildings where there were half a dozen people living in one room; people with no electricity and no heat in the dead of winter surrounded by rats, **cockroaches**(蟑螂) and the smell of **urine**(尿). It was both an astonishing realization that people lived this way and a truly fulfilling experience to make even a small difference.

You see, you can make anything happen if you commit to it and take action. Miracles like this happen every day—even in a city where "there are no vans".

61

To Any Service Member

During the Persian Gulf War, I was stationed aboard the naval **amphibious**(两栖的) ship USS Nassau. As a senior **Marine**(海军) intelligence analyst, my workdays were routinely twelve to sixteen hours long. Like all the **veterans** (老兵), we looked forward to receiving mail from home.

Unlike the Vietnam War, the Gulf War found support among most Americans. As a result, we soldiers received an enormous amount of "To any service member" mail from the States. I never took any of those letters, since I wrote to my wife and two children on a daily basis, as well as occasionally writing notes to my daughter's classroom, and I didn't feel I had time to write to anyone else.

After five or six months of hearing the mail orderly—announcing the availability of "To any service member" mail, I decided to take a few of the letters. I planned, as time permitted, to drop them a line telling them "Thanks" for their support.

I picked up three letters, and placed them in my cargo pocket and proceeded back to work. Over the next week or so, I started responding to the letters. When it came time to answer the third letter, I noticed it had no return address, but a Colorado postmark, which made me think of home. I had missed spending Thanksgiving, Christmas and New Year's with my family, and I was really lonesome for them.

I opened the card and started to read the letter enclosed. About the third or fourth sentence down, it read, "My Daddy is a Marine over there, if you see him, tell him hi and I love and miss him." This statement really touched me and made me miss my family even more. I looked down to the signature—and sat in stunned silence as tears filled my eyes.

My own daughter Chris had signed the letter.

62

The Santa Claus on the Highway

The **wipers**(刮雨器) struggled to push the heavy, wet snowflakes off the **windshield**(挡风玻璃) while they kept rhythm to Willie Nelson singing "On the Road Again".

Trint hit the **eject button**(弹出键) on the tape player. He'd heard that song four times in the last two hours and was sick of it. He shrugged his aching shoulders trying to shake off the miles. It was still a long way to Memphis, a storm was blowing in and the highway was getting **hazardous**(危险的).

In the distance, Trint saw the welcome glow of lights at a truck stop and decided to pull off the road and grab a bite to eat while he waited to see if the weather would break or turn into an icy **blizzard** (暴风雪) that would shut down the roads until morning.

He eased his orange **Freightliner**(集装箱货运车) and fifty-three-foot-long **trailer**(拖车) into an empty spot and shut it down. He was **hauling**(运送) a heavy load of tires to Nashville, and after that he was picking up a load in Baltimore and heading to Chicago.

He reached for his jacket and hesitated when he saw the box on the passenger seat. His mother had been worried about him spending

Christmas on the road alone and had given him a box filled with presents. He smiled; his Mom still treated him like he was a kid. He looked at his watch. It was nearly midnight on Christmas Eve, so he might as well open his gifts now.

Trint tore open the box and found a warm **flannel**(法兰绒) shirt, probably blue. It was hard to tell in the dim light, but his Mom knew his favorite color was blue. There were some heavy socks and leather gloves. Mom was always **fussing over**(担忧) him and worrying her youngest son would get cold. There were homemade cookies and **fudge**(软糖) and a red stocking with Santa Claus on it. He reached into the stocking and pulled out a toy tractor trailer that looked a lot like his trailer and wondered how many stores his mother had to go to before she found such a close match.

His eyes stung. Next month he'd be twenty-five years old. He was a man. Men didn't cry over cookies and a toy truck or because they were a thousand miles away from home on Christmas.

He climbed out of his cab and a cold blast of air hit him in the chest like a fist. He pulled his collar up and ran across the parking lot to the all-night cafe. He was tall and thin and without much meat on his bones to protect him from the cold. Inside, it was warm and cozy. A dozen truckers were spread out at the counter and tables. A man and woman and small boy were huddled in a room, and they looked tired and unhappy.

Trint felt sorry for the boy. He looked like he was around eight years old, and no kid should have to spend Christmas Eve in a truck stop. The parents were loading up on coffee and Trint guessed they'd been driving somewhere to spend the holidays with relatives, and the snow forced them to hole up here. They were drinking coffee hoping to stay awake so they could finish their trip if the weather cleared up.

"It's so cold outside, I was spitting ice **cubes**(块)," a fat trucker at the counter said, and the others laughed.

A cute waitress with blonde hair offered Trint a menu.

"I'll have biscuits and **gravy**(肉汤)..." he said.

"And iced tea with lemon," she finished the order for him. "You're the only trucker around here who doesn't drink coffee." She smiled and didn't seem in a hurry to leave.

"I'm surprised you remember me." Trint returned her smile.

"How could I ever forget those beautiful brown eyes and your country accent?" she asked, hoping he would guess that she watched for him every time a truck pulled in.

"Well, I remember you, too," he grinned. "You want to be school teacher, I think you said first or second grade, you're putting yourself through college by working here at night and your name is Melinda."

"You do remember!" she said, liking the soft way he said her name. Color flushed her cheeks and she hurried off into the kitchen.

Funny how truckers picked up bits and pieces of other people's lives. He looked across the room. Some of the truckers' faces looked familiar but he didn't know any of their names. He might see them again tomorrow at another truck stop, or never see them again. Sometimes his job seemed awfully lonely. Trint liked driving a truck, he liked seeing new places and he liked the good pay, but sometimes, like tonight, he felt lonesome and wondered if this was really the life for him.

He missed his family. His Mom raised four kids by herself on a forty-acre farm in Missouri but no matter how scarce money was, she'd always made sure they had a good Christmas. He thought about his box of gifts in the truck.

He looked at the kid again and knew what he had to do. He forced himself back into the bone-chilling cold outside to walk to his truck. He grabbed the Christmas stocking out of the cab and hurried back to the warmth of the cafe.

He walked to the room where the family sat in weary silence.

"I think Santa Claus left this for you," Trint said and handed the red stocking to the boy.

The boy looked at his mother. She hesitated just a second and

135

nodded. The boy eagerly reached out and took the stocking and dug inside.

"Wow! Mom, look! A big trailer just like the real ones outside!" His grin lit up the whole room.

"Tell Santa... well, tell him thanks," the boy's father said and shook Trint's hand long and hard. The mother smiled gratefully.

Trint returned to the counter and ate his biscuits and gravy. He gave the waitress a twenty-dollar **tip**（小费）and told her merry Christmas. She said the money was too much, but he told her to use it to buy some books for school, and she took it and slipped him a piece of paper.

"Take good care of yourself," she said. "And hurry back."

"I will . . . Melinda," he promised and noticed she had the bluest eyes he'd ever seen.

Trint walked outside. It had stopped snowing and a handful of stars sparkled through a break in the clouds.

There was a tap on the window behind him and he turned to look. It was the boy. He was holding up the truck and laughing. Trint waved goodbye, and the boy waved back.

Trint felt good. Somewhere along the road tomorrow he'd call home and talk to his brothers and kid sister. He'd tell his Mom about giving the toy to the kid. She'd like that.

Trint reached his truck and stopped. Somebody had written "Merry X-mas," in the snow on his windshield and hung a candy cane on his side mirror. He wondered if it was Melinda or the boy or one of the truckers.

He started up his engine and felt the roar and power as he slowly pulled up to the road. Soon the **snowplows**(扫雪机) would be out and clear the snow on the highway, but right now the road stretched out like a silver ribbon.

A quiet peace filled Trint's heart. He was a lucky guy. He had a job he loved, Melinda's phone number in his pocket, clear weather and miles of open road ahead.

He wasn't tired anymore, or lonely. He loved this life and he wouldn't change a thing.

63

The Fortune Cookie Prophecy

I was married three times before I was seven years old.

My older brother Gary performed the ceremonies in our basement. Gary was good at entertaining the family and neighborhood kids with his creative ideas. Since I was the youngest boy in our group, I was often on the receiving end of his creativity.

What I remember most about those weddings is that all the girls were at least five years older than I was, and they all had beautiful eyes that sparkled when they laughed. Those weddings taught me to imagine what it would be like to find my soul mate one day and to be sure that I would know her by her beautiful eyes.

Puberty(青春期) hit me late. I was still afraid of the opposite sex when I was fifteen, and yet I prayed every night for the girl I would marry. I asked God to help her do well in school and to be happy and full of energy—wherever and whoever she was.

I first kissed a girl when I was twenty-one. From that time forward, I dated many beautiful and talented young ladies, searching for the girl I had prayed for in my youth and still certain that I would know her by her eyes.

One day, my phone rang. "Don," it was my mother. "You know I told you about the Addisons, who moved in next door to us. Well, Clara Addison keeps asking me to invite you over for cards some night."

"Sorry, Mom, I've got a date that night."

"How could you? I haven't even told you what night it is?" my mother responded with **exasperation**(恼怒).

"It doesn't matter when. I'm sure the Addisons are nice people, but I'm not going to waste an evening socializing with people who don't have any **eligible**(合适的) daughters."

That's how stubborn I was—I was positive that there was no reason for me to go to visit the Addisons.

Years passed. I was twenty-six, and my friends were getting nervous about my prospects. They kept lining up blind dates for me. Many of these dates were **fiascoes**(惨败), and they were interfering with my social life. So I made up a few rules about blind dates:

1) No dates recommended by my mother (moms don't understand the sex-appeal factor)

2) No dates recommended by a female (they're too easy on each other)

3) No dates recommended by a single guy friend (if she's so good, how come he hasn't asked her out?)

In three simple steps, I **eliminated**(排除) 90 percent of all my blind dates, including one recommended by my old friend Karen. She called one evening to tell me that she had become good friends with a beautiful girl who reminded her of me. She said she knew we would **hit it off**(合得来).

"Sorry," I said, "you're ruled out by rule number two."

"Don," she said, "you're crazy, and your silly rules are eliminating the girl you've been waiting for. But have it your way. Just take her name and phone number, and when you change your mind, call her."

To get Karen to stop bothering me about it, I said I would. The girl's name was Susan Maready. I never called her.

Just a couple of weeks later, I ran into my old buddy Ted in the university cafeteria.

"Ted," I said. "You look like you're **walking on air**(洋洋得意)."

"Can you see stars under my feet?" he said, laughing. "The fact is, I just got engaged last night."

"Hey, **congratulations**(恭喜)!"

"Yeah," he said, "at thirty-two, I was beginning to wonder if any woman was going to have me." He pulled his wallet out of his pocket. "Here," he said, suddenly serious, "look at this."

It was a thin strip of paper from a **fortune cookie**(幸运饼干). "You will be married within a year," it said.

"That's wild," I said. "They usually say something that would fit anyone, like 'You have a magnetic personality'. They were really **taking a chance**(冒险) with that one."

"No kidding," he said. "And look at me now."

A few weeks later, my roommate Charlie and I were eating dinner at a Chinese restaurant. I shared this story about Ted's fortune cookie prediction, and his subsequent engagement. Just then, the waiter brought over our postmeal fortune cookies. Charlie laughed at the coincidence as we opened our cookies. Mine said, "You have a magnetic personality." His said, "You or a close friend will be married within a year." A chill ran up my **spine**(脊椎). This was really strange. Something told me to ask Charlie if I could keep his fortune, and he handed it to me with a smile.

Not long afterward, my classmate Brian said he wanted to introduce me to a young woman named Susan Maready. I was sure I'd heard that name before, but couldn't remember how or where. Since Brian was married, and therefore I wouldn't be breaking my "rules" about being fixed up by single guys, I accepted his offer to meet Susan.

Susan and I spoke on the phone, and planned a bike ride and a cookout. Then, the meeting—and as soon as I saw her, my heart started beating hard and wouldn't stop. Her large green eyes did something to me I couldn't explain. But somewhere in me, I knew that it was love at first sight.

After that wonderful evening, I remembered that this hadn't been the first time someone tried to fix me up with Susan. It all came back

to me. Her name had been popping up all over the place for a long time. So the next time I had a chance to talk to Brian alone, I asked him about it. He **squirmed**(难为情) and tried to change the subject.

"What is it, Brian?" I asked.

"You'll have to ask Susan," was all he'd say.

So I did.

"I was going to tell you," she said. "I was going to tell you."

"Come on, Susan," I said. "Tell me what? I can't stand the **suspense**(悬念)."

"I've been in love with you for years," she said, "since the first time I saw you from the Addisons' living room window. Yes, it was me they wanted you to meet. But you wouldn't let anyone introduce us. You wouldn't let the Addisons set us up; you wouldn't take Karen's word for it that we would like each other. I thought I was never going to meet you."

My heart swelled with love, and I laughed at myself. "Karen was right," I said. "My rules were crazy."

"You're not mad?" she asked.

"Are you kidding?" I said. "I'm impressed. I've got only one rule for blind dating now."

She gave me a strange look. "What's that?"

"Never again," I said and kissed her.

We were married seven months later.

Susan and I are convinced that we are true soul mates. When I was fifteen and praying for my future wife, she was fourteen and praying for her future husband.

After we had been married a couple of months, Susan said to me, "Do you want to hear something really strange?"

"Sure," I said. "I love to hear strange things."

"Well, about ten months ago, before I'd met you, my friends and I were at this Chinese restaurant, and…" She pulled a slip of paper from a fortune cookie out of her wallet:

"You will be married within a year…"

64

A Coke and a Smile

I know now that the man who sat with me on the old wooden stairs that hot summer night over thirty-five years ago was not a tall man. But to a five-year-old, he was a giant. We sat side by side, watching the sun go down behind the old Texaco service station across the busy street. A street that I was never allowed to cross unless accompanied by an adult, or at the very least, an older brother or sister. An unlikely pair, we sat together on the top step. His legs reached down two stairs; mine angled, barely reaching the first. The night was **muggy**(闷热) and the air thick. It was the summer of 1959.

Cherry-scented smoke from Grandpa's pipe **kept the hungry mosquitoes at bay**(把蚊子驱开) while gray, **wispy swirls**(小飞虫) danced around our heads. Now and again, he blew a smoke ring and laughed as I tried to target the hole with my finger. I, dressed in a cool summer shirt, and Grandpa, his sleeveless T-shirt, sat watching the traffic, trying to catch the elusive breeze. We counted cars and tried to guess the color of the next one to turn the corner. I was luckier at this game than Grandpa.

Once again, I was caught in the middle of circumstances. The

141

fourth born of six children, it was not uncommon that I was either too young or too old for something. This night I was both. While my two baby brothers slept inside the house, my three older brothers and sisters played with friends around the corner, where I was not allowed to go. I stayed with Grandpa, and that was okay with me. I was where I wanted to be. My grandpa was baby-sitting while my mother, father and grandmother went out.

"Thirsty?" Grandpa asked, never removing the pipe from his mouth.

"Yes," was my reply.

"How would you like to run over to the gas station there and get yourself a bottle of Coke?"

I couldn't believe my ears. Had I heard right? Was he talking to me? On my family's modest income, Coke was not a part of our **budget**(预算) or diet. A few **tantalizing**(诱人的) **sips**(小口喝) was all I had ever had, and certainly never my own bottle.

"Okay," I replied shyly, already wondering how I would get across the street. Surely Grandpa was going to come with me.

Grandpa stretched his long leg out straight and reached his huge hand deep into the pocket. I could hear the familiar jangling of the loose change he always carried. Opening his fist, he exposed a mound of silver coins. There must have been a million dollars there. He instructed me to pick out a dime. I obeyed. After he put the rest of the change back into his pocket, he stood up.

"Okay," he said, helping me down the stairs and to the **curb**(边石) of the street, "I'm going to stay here and keep an ear out for the babies. I'll tell you when it's safe to cross. You go over to the Coke machine, get your Coke and come back out. Wait for me to tell you when it's safe to cross back."

My heart pounded. I clutched my dime tightly in my sweaty hand. Excitement took my breath away.

Grandpa held my hand tightly. Together we looked up the street and down, and back up again. He stepped off the curb and told me it

was safe to cross. He let go of my hand and I ran. I ran faster than I had ever run before. The street seemed wide. I wondered if I would make it to the other side. Reaching the other side, I turned to find Grandpa. There he was, standing exactly where I had left him, smiling proudly. I waved.

"Go on, hurry up," he yelled.

My heart pounded wildly as I walked inside the dark garage. I had been inside the garage before with my father. My surroundings were familiar. My eyes adjusted, and I heard the Coca-Cola machine motor humming even before I saw it. I walked directly to the big old red-and-white **dispenser**(自动售货机). I knew where to insert my dime. I had seen it done before and had **fantasized**(幻想) about this moment many times. I checked over my shoulder. Grandpa waved.

The big old **monster**(怪物) greedily accepted my dime, and I heard the bottles shift. On tiptoes I reached up and opened the heavy door. There they were: one neat row of thick green bottles, necks staring directly at me, and ice-cold from the **refrigeration**(冷藏). I held the door open with my shoulder and grabbed one. With a quick **yank**(猛拉), I pulled it free from its **bondage**(束缚). Another one immediately took its place. The bottle was cold in my sweaty hands.

I will never forget the feeling of the cool glass on my skin. With two hands, I positioned the bottleneck under the heavy **brass**(铜) opener that was **bolted**(闩) to the wall. The cap dropped into an old wooden box, and I reached in to get it. I was cold and bent in the middle, but I knew I needed to have this **souvenir**(纪念品). Coke in hand, I proudly marched back out into the early evening dusk. Grandpa was waiting patiently. He smiled.

"Stop right there," he yelled. One or two cars sped by me, and once again, Grandpa stepped off the curb.

"Come on, now," he said, "run." I did. Cool brown **foam**(泡沫) sprayed my hands. Soon I came back to my Grandpa.

"Don't ever do that alone," he warned firmly.

"Never," I assured him.

I held the Coke bottle tightly, fearful he would make me pour it into a cup, ruining this dream come true. He didn't. One long swallow of the cold drink cooled my sweating body. I don't think I ever felt so proud.

There we sat, side by side, watching the sun go down behind the old Texaco service station across the busy street. A street I had been allowed to cross by myself.

Grandpa stretched his long legs down over two stairs. I **dangled** (悬吊) mine, a bit closer to the first step this time, I'm sure.

65

The Best Time of My Life

It was June 15, and in two days I would be turning thirty. I was not sure about entering a new decade of my life and feared that my best years were now behind me.

My daily routine included going to the gym for a workout before going to work. Every morning I would see my friend Nicholas at the gym. He was seventy-nine years old and **in terrific shape**(非常健康). As I greeted Nicholas on this particular day, he noticed I wasn't full of my usual **vitality**(活力) and asked if there was anything wrong. I told him I was feeling anxious about turning thirty. I wondered how I would look back on my life once I reached Nicholas's age, so I asked him, "What was the best time of your life?"

Without hesitation, Nicholas replied, "Well, Joe, this is my philosophical answer to your philosophical question:

"When I was a child in Austria and everything was taken care of for me and I was **nurtured**(养育) by my parents, that was the best time of my life.

"When I was going to school and learning the things I know today, that was the best time of my life.

"When I got my first job and had responsibilities and got paid for my efforts, that was the best time of my life.

"When I met my wife and fell in love, that was the best time of my life.

"The Second World War came, and my wife and I had to flee Austria to save our lives. When we were together and safe on a ship bound for North America, that was the best time of my life.

"When we came to Canada and started a family, that was the best time of my life.

"When I was a young father, watching my children grow up, that was the best time of my life.

"And now, Joe, I am seventy-nine years old. I have my health, I feel good and I am in love with my wife just as I was when we first met. This is the best time of my life."

66

The Easter Bunny

When I was a little girl, every Sunday my family of six would put on our best clothes and go to Sunday School and then church. The kids in elementary school would all meet together to sing songs, and then later divide into groups based on their ages.

One Easter Sunday, all the kids arrived with big eyes and big stories about what the Easter **Bunny**(兔) had brought. While all of the kids shared their stories with delight, one young boy, whom I will call Bobby, sat **sullenly**(闷闷不乐). One of the teachers, noticing this, said to him, "And what did the Easter Bunny bring you?"

He replied, "My mom locked the door on accident so the Easter Bunny couldn't get inside."

This sounded like a reasonable idea to all of us kids, so we kept on going with the stories. My mom knew the true story, though. Bobby's mom was a single parent, and she thought that they just couldn't afford the Easter Bunny.

After Sunday School was over, everyone went off to church. When my dad came to meet us, my mom announced that we were going home instead. At home, she explained that to make Bobby feel better, we were going to pretend to be the Easter Bunny and make a basket of **goodies**(好吃的) for him and leave it at church. We all donated some of our candies to the basket, and headed back up to church. There, mom **unzipped**(拉开拉链) the coat, hung the basket over the hanger, and zipped up the coat and attached a note:

Dear Bobby,
I'm sorry I missed your house last night. Happy Easter.
Love,
Easter Bunny

67

Cyber Step-Mother

I've often felt that "step-parent" is a label we attach to men and women who marry into families where children already exist, for the simple reason that we need to call them something. It is most certainly an enormous "step", but one doesn't often feel as if the term "parent" truly applies. At least that's how I used to feel about being a step-mother to my husband's four children.

My husband and I had been together for six years, and with him I had watched as his young children became young teenagers. Although they lived primarily with their mother, they spent a lot of time with us as well. Over the years, we all learned to adjust, to become more comfortable with each other, and to **adapt to**(适应) our new family arrangement. We enjoyed holidays together, ate family meals, worked on homework, played baseball, rented videos. However, I continued to feel somewhat like an outsider, **infringing upon**(侵占) foreign territory. There was a definite boundary line that could not be crossed, an inner family circle which excluded me. Since I had no children of my own, my experience of parenting was limited to my husband's four, and often I **lamented**(伤心) that I would never know the special bond that exists between a parent and a child.

When the children moved to a town five hours away, my husband was understandably **devastated**(受摧残的). In order to maintain regular communication with the kids, we contacted **Cyberspace**(网络通信) and at once set up an e-mail and chat-line service. This technology, combined with the telephone, would enable us to reach them on a daily basis by sending frequent notes and messages, and even chatting together when we were all on-line.

Ironically(具有反讽意味地), these modern tools of communication can also be tools of **alienation**(疏远), making us feel so out of touch, so much more in need of real human contact. If a computer message came addressed to "Dad", I'd feel forgotten and neglected. If my name appeared along with his, it would brighten my day and make me feel like I was part of their family unit after all. Yet always there was some distance to be crossed, not just over the telephone wires.

Late one evening, as my husband **snoozed**(打瞌睡) in front of the television and I was catching up on my e-mail, an "instant message" appeared on the screen. It was Margo, my oldest step-daughter, also up late and sitting in front of her computer five hours away. As we had done in the past, we sent several messages back and forth, exchanging

the latest news. When we would "chat" like that, she wouldn't necessarily know if it was me or her dad on the other end of the keyboard—that is unless she asked. That night she didn't ask and I didn't identify myself either. After hearing the latest volleyball scores, the details about an upcoming dance at her school, and a history project that was in the works, I said that it was late and I should get to sleep. Her return message read, "Okay, talk to you later! Love you!"

As I read this message, a wave of sadness ran through me and I realized that she must have thought she was writing to her father the whole time. She and I would never have openly exchanged such words of affection. Feeling guilty for not clarifying, yet not wanting to embarrass her, I simply returned the answer, "Love you too! Have a good sleep!"

I thought again of their family circle, that self-contained, private space where I was an **intruder**(闯入者). I felt again the sharp ache of emptiness and otherness. Then, just as my fingers reached for the keys, just as I was about to return the screen to black, Margo's final message appeared. It read, "Tell Dad good night for me, too."

With tear-filled, blurry eyes, I turned the machine off.

68

The Pickle Jar

As far back as I can remember, the large **pickle jar**(泡菜坛) sat on the floor beside the dresser in my parents' bedroom. When he got ready for bed, Dad would empty his pockets and toss his coins into the jar. As a small boy I was always **fascinated**(着迷) at the sounds the coins made as they were dropped into the jar. They landed with a merry jingle when the jar was almost empty. Then the tones gradually

muted to a dull **thud**(撞击声) as the jar was filled. I used to squat on the floor in front of the jar and admire the copper and silver circles that **glinted**(闪光) like a pirate's treasure when the sun poured through the bedroom window.

When the jar was filled, Dad would sit at the kitchen table and roll the coins in pieces of paper before taking them to the bank. Taking the coins to the bank was always a big production. **Stacked**(堆) neatly in a small cardboard box, the coins were placed between Dad and me on the seat of his old truck. Each and every time, as we drove to the bank, Dad would look at me hopefully.

"Those coins are going to keep you out of the **textile mill**(纺织厂), son. You're going to do better than me. This old mill town is not going to hold you back."

Also, each and every time, as he slid the box of rolled coins across the counter at the bank toward the **cashier**(出纳员), he would grin proudly. "These are for my son's college fund. He'll never work at the mill all his life like me."

We would always celebrate each **deposit**(存款) by stopping for an ice cream cone. I always got chocolate. Dad always got **vanilla**(香草味). When the clerk at the ice cream parlor handed Dad his change, he would show me the few coins nestled in his palm. "When we get home, we'll start filling the jar again."

He always let me drop the first coins into the empty jar. As they rattled around with a brief, happy jingle, we grinned at each other.

"You'll get to college on pennies, nickels, dimes and quarters," he said. "But you'll get there. I'll see to that."

The years passed, and I finished college and took a job in another town. Once, while visiting my parents, I used the phone in their bedroom, and noticed that the pickle jar was gone. It had served its purpose and had been removed. A lump rose in my throat as I stared at the spot beside the dresser where the jar had always stood. My Dad was a man of few words, and never lectured me on the values of **determination**(决心), **perseverance**(坚持), and faith. The pickle

jar had taught me all these **virtues**(美德)far more eloquently than the most flowery of words could have done.

When I married, I told my wife Susan about the significant part the lowly pickle jar had played in my life as a boy. In my mind, it defined, more than anything else, how much my Dad had loved me. No matter how rough things got at home, Dad continued to **doggedly**(顽强地) drop his coins into the jar. Even the summer when Dad lost his job from the mill, and Mama had to serve dried beans several times a week, not a single dime was taken from the jar. To the contrary, as Dad looked across the table at me, pouring **catsup**(番茄酱) over my beans to make them more **palatable**(可口的), he became more determined than ever to make a way out for me.

"When you finish college, son," he told me, his eyes glistening, "you'll never have to eat beans again unless you want to."

The first Christmas after our daughter Jessica was born, we spent the holiday with my parents. After dinner, Mom and Dad sat next to each other on the sofa, taking turns **cuddling**(怀抱) their first grandchild. Jessica began to whimper softly, and Susan took her from Dad's arms.

"She probably needs to be changed," she said, carrying the baby into my parents' bedroom to **diaper**(换尿布) her.

When Susan came back into the living room, there was a strange mist in her eyes. She handed Jessica back to Dad before taking my hand and quietly leading me into the room.

"Look," she said softly, her eyes directing me to a spot on the floor beside the dresser. To my amazement, there, as if it had never been removed, stood the old pickle jar, the bottom already covered with coins.

I walked over to the pickle jar, dug down into my pocket, and pulled out a fistful of coins. With **a gamut of emotions**(百感交集) choking me, I dropped the coins into the jar. I looked up and saw that Dad, carrying Jessica, had slipped quietly into the room. Our eyes locked, and I knew he was feeling the same emotions I felt. Neither one of us could speak.

69

Late for School

All my life, I've had this **recurring**(重复的) dream that causes me to wake up feeling strange. In it, I am a little girl again, rushing about, trying to get ready for school.

"Hurry, Gin, you'll be late for school," my mother calls to me.

"I am hurrying, Mom! Where's my lunch? What did I do with my books?"

Deep inside I know where the dream comes from and what it means. It is God's way of reminding me of some unfinished business in my life.

I loved everything about school, even though the school I attended in Springfield, Ohio, in the 1920s was very strict. I loved books, teachers, even tests and homework. Most of all I longed to someday march down the aisle to the **strains**(乐曲) of "**Pomp and Circumstance**"(毕业盛典). To me, that song was even more beautiful than "Here Comes the Bride."

But there were problems.

The Great Depression(经济大萧条) hit the hardest at large, poor families like ours. With seven children, Mom and Dad had no

money for things like fine school clothes. Every morning, I cut out strips of cardboard to stuff inside my shoes to cover the holes in the **soles**(鞋底). There was no money for musical instruments or sports uniforms or after-school treats. We sang to ourselves, played **jacks**(抓子游戏) or duck-on-the-rock, and **munched**(咀嚼) on onions as we did homework.

These hardships I accepted. As long as I could go to school, I didn't mind too much how I looked or what I lacked.

What happened next was harder to accept. My brother Paul died of an infection after he accidentally stabbed himself in the eye with a fork. Then my father **contracted tuberculosis**(患上肺结核) and died. My sister, Margaret, caught the same disease, and soon she was gone, too.

The shock of these losses gave me an **ulcer**(溃疡), and I fell behind in my schoolwork. Meanwhile, my widowed mother tried to keep going on the five dollars a week she made cleaning houses. Her face became a mask of despair.

One day I said to her, "Mom, I'm going to **quit school**(辍学) and get a job to help out."

The look in her eyes was a mixture of grief and relief.

At fifteen, I dropped out of my beloved school and went to work in a bakery. My hope of walking down the aisle to "Pomp and Circumstance" was dead, or so I thought.

In 1940, I married Ed, a **machinist**(机械工), and we began our family. Then Ed decided to become a **preacher**(传道士), so we moved to Cincinnati where he could attend the Cincinnati Bible Seminary. With the coming of children went the dream of schooling, forever.

Even so, I was determined that my children would have the education I had missed. I made sure the house was filled with books and magazines. I helped them with their homework and urged them to study hard. It paid off. All our six children eventually got some college training, and one of them is a college professor.

But Linda, our last child, had health problems. Juvenile arthritis in her hands and knees made it impossible for her to study in the typical classroom. Furthermore, the **medications**(药物) gave her **cramps**(抽筋), stomach trouble and **migraine headaches**(偏头痛).

Teachers and principals were not always sympathetic. I lived in dread of the phone calls from school. "Mom, I'm coming home."

Now Linda was nineteen, and still she did not have her high school **diploma**(毕业证). She was repeating my own experience.

I prayed about this problem, and when we moved to Sturgis, Michigan, in 1979, I began to see an answer. I drove to the local high school to check it out. On the bulletin board, I saw an announcement about evening courses.

That's the answer, I said to myself. Linda always feels better in the evening, so I'll just sign her up for night school.

Linda was busy filling out **enrollment**(注册) forms when the **registrar**(注册主任) looked at me with brown, persuasive eyes and said, "Mrs. Schantz, why don't you come back to school?"

I laughed in his face. "Me? Ha! I'm an old woman. I'm fifty-five!"

But he persisted, and before I knew what I had done, I was enrolled for classes in English and **crafts**(工艺).

"This is only an experiment," I warned him, but he just smiled.

To my surprise, both Linda and I did well in evening school. I went back again the next semester, and my grades steadily improved.

It was exciting, going to school again, but it was no game. Sitting in a class full of kids was awkward, but most of them were respectful and encouraging. During the day, I still had loads of housework to do and grandchildren to care for. Sometimes, I stayed up until two in the morning, adding columns of numbers for bookkeeping class. When the numbers didn't seem to work out, my eyes would cloud with tears and I would **berate**(训斥)myself, "Why am I so dumb?"

But when I was down, Linda encouraged me. "Mom, you can't quit now!" And when she was down, I encouraged her. Together we

would see this through.

At last, graduation was near, and the registrar called me into his office. I entered, trembling, afraid I had done something wrong.

He smiled and motioned for me to have a seat. "Mrs. Schantz," he began, "you have done very well in school."

I blushed with relief.

"As a matter of fact," he went on, "your classmates have **voted unanimously**(全票通过) for you to be **class orator**(毕业典礼发言人)."

I was speechless.

He smiled again and handed me a piece of paper. "And here is a little reward for all your hard work."

I looked at the paper. It was a college scholarship for $3,000. "Thank you" was all I could think to say, and I said it over and over.

The night of graduation, I was terrified. Two hundred people were sitting out there, and public speaking was a brand-new experience for me. My mouth **wrinkled**(皱起来) as if I had been eating **persimmons**(柿子).

My heart skipped beats, and I wanted to flee, but I couldn't! After all, my own children were sitting in that audience. I couldn't be a **coward**(懦夫) in front of them.

Then, when I heard the first strains of "Pomp and Circumstance," my fears **dissolved**(消除) in a flood of delight. I am graduating! And so is Linda!

Somehow I got through the speech. I was startled by the applause, the first I ever remember receiving in my life.

Afterwards, roses arrived from my brothers and sisters throughout the Midwest. My husband gave me silk roses, "So they will not fade."

The local **media**(媒体) showed up with cameras and recorders and lots of questions. There were tears and hugs and congratulations. I was proud of Linda, and a little afraid that I might have unintentionally stolen some of the attention that she deserved for her victory, but she seemed as proud as anyone of our dual success.

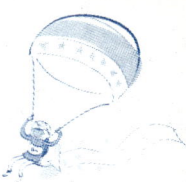

The class of '81 is history now, and I've gone on for some college education. But sometimes, I sit down and put on the tape of my graduation speech. I hear myself say to the audience, "Don't ever **underestimate**(低估) your dreams in life. Anything can happen if you believe. Not a childish, magical belief. It means hard work, but never doubt that you can do it, with God's help."

And then, I remember the recurring dream—"Hurry, Gin, you'll be late for school." And my eyes cloud over when I think of my mother.

Yes, Mom, I was late for school, but it was all the sweeter for waiting. I only wish you and Dad could have been there to see your daughter and granddaughter in all their pomp and circumstance.

70

Stepfather's Day

With Father's Day coming up, it occurred to me that this country is missing a holiday, Stepfather's Day.

If anyone deserves a special day, it's these brave souls who've had to carve out a place for themselves in ready-made families with the care and caution of a **neuro-surgeon**(神经科医生).

That's why we have a Bobber's Day in our family. It's our own version of Stepfather's Day, named after Bob the stepfather. Here's why we celebrate it.

The Bobber has just moved in our house.

"If you do anything to hurt my mother, I could put you in the hospital, you know," says the college boy, who is far bigger than the stepfather.

"I'll keep that in mind," says the Bobber.

"You're not going to start telling me what to do," says the junior-high schoolboy. "You aren't my father."

"I'll keep that in mind," says the Bobber.

The college boy is on the phone. His car has broken down forty-five miles from home.

"I'll be right there," says the Bobber.

The vice principal is on the phone. The junior schoolboy has been in a fight.

"I'll be right there," says the Bobber.

"I need a tie to go with this shirt," says the college boy.

"Pick one out of my closet," says the Bobber.

"You need to get your ear **pierced**(穿孔)," says the junior schoolboy.

"You need to stop **burping**(打嗝) at the table," says the Bobber.

"I'll try," says the boy.

"I'll think about it," says the Bobber.

"What did you think of my date last night?" asks the college boy.

"Does it make a difference?" asks the Bobber.

"Yes," says the boy.

"I need to talk to you," says the junior schoolboy.

"I need to talk to you," says the Bobber.

"We should have a stepfather-stepson bonding experience," says the college boy.

"Doing what?" asks the Bobber.

"Changing the oil in my car," says the boy.

"I knew it," says the Bobber.

"We should have a stepfather-stepson bonding experience," says the junior schoolboy.

"Doing what?" asks the Bobber.

"Driving me to the movies," says the boy.

"I knew it," says the Bobber.

"If you drink, don't get in the car. Call me," says the Bobber.

"Thanks," says the college boy.

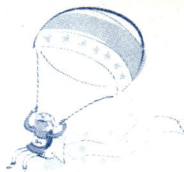

"If you drink, don't get in the car. Call me," says the college boy.

"Thanks," says the Bobber.

"What time do I have to be home?" asks the junior schoolboy.

"11:30," says the Bobber.

"Okay," says the boy.

"Don't ever do anything to hurt him," the college boy says to me. "We need him."

"I'll keep that in mind," I say.

And so we have Bobber's Day. The boys buy their stepfather a new toy they can all play with. The Bobber **grills**(烤) steaks. And I am awed by our great fortune that the Bobber earned his way into this family with such **grace**(魅力) that it now seems he was always there.

71

Humor Them

One of the requirements of every commencement speaker is that they offer some advice. Well, get ready, here it comes.

Soon you will be leaving the company of those who think they have all the answers—your professors, instructors and counselors—and going out into what we like to call the real world. In time you will meet up with other people who think they have all the answers. These people are called bosses. My advice is: **humor**(迁就) them.

A little later you will meet additional people who think they have all the answers. These are called **spouses**(配偶). My advice is: humor them, too.

And if all goes well, in a few years you will meet still another group of people who think they have all the answers. These are called children. Humor them.

Life will go on, your children will grow up, go to school, and someday they could be taking part in a commencement ceremony just like this one. And who knows, the speaker responsible for handing out good advice might be you. Halfway through your speech, the graduate sitting next to your daughter will lean over and ask, "Who is that woman up there who thinks she has all the answers?"

Well, thanks to the sound advice you are hearing today and that I hope you will all pass on, she will be able to say, "That is my mother. Humor her."

72
Who You Are Makes a Difference

A teacher in New York decided to **honor**(向……表示敬意) each of her seniors in high school by telling them the difference they each made. Using a process developed by Helice Bridges of Del Mar, California, she called each student to the front of the class, one at a time. First she told them how the student made a difference to her and the class. Then she presented each of them with a blue ribbon imprinted with gold letters which read, "Who I Am Makes a Difference."

Afterwards the teacher decided to do a class project to see what kind of impact recognition would have on a community. She gave each of the students three more ribbons and instructed them to go out and spread this acknowledgment ceremony. Then they were to follow up on the results, see who honored whom and report back to the class in about a week.

One of the boys in the class went to a junior executive in a nearby company and honored him for helping him with his career planning. He

gave him a blue ribbon and put it on his shirt. Then he gave him two extra ribbons, and said, "We're doing a class project on recognition, and we'd like you to go out, find somebody to honor, give them a blue ribbon, then give them the extra blue ribbon so they can acknowledge a third person to keep this acknowledgment ceremony going. Then please report back to me and tell me what happened."

Later that day the junior executive went in to see his boss, who had been noted, by the way, as being kind of a **grouchy**(坏脾气) fellow. He sat his boss down and he told him that he deeply admired him for being a creative genius. The boss seemed very surprised. The junior executive asked him if he would accept the gift of the blue ribbon and give him permission to put it on him. His surprised boss said, "Well, sure."

The junior executive took the blue ribbon and placed it right on his boss' jacket above his heart. As he gave him the last extra ribbon, he said, "Would you do me a favor? Would you take this extra ribbon and pass it on by honoring somebody else? The young boy who first gave me the ribbons is doing a project in school and we want to keep this recognition ceremony going and find out how it affects people."

That night the boss came home to his 14-year-old son and sat him down. He said, "The most incredible thing happened to me today. I was in my office and one of the junior executives came in and told me he admired me and gave me a blue ribbon for being a creative genius. Imagine. He thinks I'm a creative genius. Then he put this blue ribbon that says 'Who I Am Makes a Difference' on my jacket above my heart. He gave me an extra ribbon and asked me to find somebody else to honor. As I was driving home tonight, I started thinking about whom I would honor with this ribbon and I thought about you. I want to honor you.

"My days are really **hectic**(忙乱的) and when I come home I don't pay a lot of attention to you. Sometimes I scream at you for not getting good enough grades in school and for your bedroom being a mess, but somehow tonight, I just wanted to sit here and well, just let you know

that you do make a difference to me. Besides your mother, you are the most important person in my life. You're a great kid and I love you!"

The surprised boy started to **sob**(啜泣) and sob, and he couldn't stop crying. His whole body shook. He looked up at his father and said through his tears, "I was planning on **committing suicide**(自杀) tomorrow, Dad, because I didn't think you loved me. Now I don't need to."

73

Jessie's Glove

I do a lot of management training each year for the Circle K Corporation, a national chain of convenience stores. Among the topics we address in our **seminars**(研讨班) is the **retention**(留住) of quality employees—a real challenge to managers when you consider the **pay scale**(工资级别) in the service industry. During these discussions, I ask the participants, "What has caused you to stay long enough to become a manager?" Some time back a new manager, with the name Cynthia, took the question and slowly, with her voice almost breaking, said, "It was a $19 baseball glove."

Cynthia told the group that she originally took a Circle K clerk job as an **interim**(临时的) position while she looked for something better. On her second or third day behind the counter, she received a phone call from her nine-year-old son, Jessie. He needed a baseball glove for Little League. She explained that as a single mother, money was very tight, and her first check would have to go for paying bills. Perhaps she could buy his baseball glove with her second or third check.

When Cynthia arrived for work the next morning, Patricia, the store manager, asked her to come to the small room in back of the store that served as an office. Cynthia wondered if she had done something wrong or left some part of her job incomplete from the day before. She was concerned and worried.

Patricia handed her a box. "I **overheard**(偶然听到) you talking to your son yesterday," she said, "and I know that it is hard to explain things to kids. This is a baseball glove for Jessie because he may not understand how important he is, even though you have to pay bills before you can buy gloves. You know we can't pay good people like you as much as we would like to; but we do care, and I want you to know you are important to us."

The thoughtfulness, **empathy** (同情心) and love of this convenience store manager demonstrates vividly that people remember more how much an employer cares than how much the employer pays. An important lesson for the price of a Little League baseball glove.

74

A Simple Act of Love

When I was growing up, my father always stopped what he was doing and listened while I'd breathlessly fill him in on my day. For him, no subject was **off-limits**(被禁止的). When I was a **lanky**(瘦高) and awkward 13-year-old girl, Dad coached me on how to stand and walk like a lady. At 17 and madly in love, I sought his advice on **pursuing** (追求) a new student at school.

"Keep the conversation **neutral**(中性的)," he counseled. "And ask him about his car."

I followed his suggestions and gave him daily progress reports: "Terry walked me to my locker!" "Guess what? Terry held my hand!" "Dad! He asked me out!"

161

Terry and I went steady for over a year, and soon Dad was joking, "I can tell you how to get a man; the hard part is getting rid of him."

By the time I graduated from college, I was ready to spread my wings. I got a job teaching special education at a school in Coachella, California, a desert town about 170 miles from home. It was no dream job. Low-income housing across the street from the school was a **haven**(安全港) for drug users. **Street gangs**(黑帮) hung around the school after dark. Many of my charges, emotionally disturbed 10 to 14-year-old boys, had been arrested for shoplifting, car theft or **arson**(纵火).

"Be careful," Dad warned me during one of my frequent weekend visits home.

He was concerned about my living alone, but I was 23, enthusiastic and **naive**(单纯), and I needed to be on my own. Besides, teaching jobs were tight in 1974, and I felt lucky to have one.

"Don't worry," I reassured him, as I loaded up the car to start my trip back to the desert and my job.

Several evenings later I stayed after school to rearrange my classroom. After it was finished, I turned out the light and closed the door. Then I headed toward the gate. It was locked! I looked around. Everyone—teachers, **custodians**(管理员), secretaries, had gone home and, not realizing I was still there, **stranded**(使……搁浅) me on the school grounds. I glanced at my watch—it was almost 6 p.m. I had been so **engrossed**(专心) in my work that I hadn't noticed the time.

After checking all the exits, I found just enough room to squeeze under a gate in the back of the school. I pushed my purse through first, lay on my back and slowly edged through.

I retrieved my purse and walked toward my car, parked in a field behind the building. **Eerie**(可怕的) shadows fell across the schoolyard.

Suddenly, I heard voices. I glanced around and saw at least eight high-school-age boys following me. They were half a block away. Even in the near darkness I could see they were wearing gang **insignia**

(标志).

"Hey!" one called out. "You a teacher?"

"Nah, she's too young—must be an **aide**(助手)!" another said.

As I walked faster, they continued taunting me. "Hey! She's kind of cute!"

Quickening my pace, I reached into my shoulder bag to get my key ring. If I have the keys in my hands, I thought, I can unlock the car and get in before...My heart was pounding.

Frantically(发狂地), I felt all over the inside of my handbag. But the key ring wasn't there!

"Hey! Let's get the lady!" one boy shouted.

Dear Lord, please help me, I prayed silently. Suddenly, my fingers wrapped around a loose key in my purse. I didn't even know if it was for my car, but I took it out and clutched it firmly.

I jogged across the grass to my car and tried the key. It worked! I opened the door, slid in and locked it—just as the teenagers surrounded the car, kicking the sides and banging on the roof. Trembling, I started the engine and drove away.

Later, some teachers went back to the school with me. With flashlights, we found the key ring on the ground by the gate, where it had fallen as I slid through.

When I returned to my apartment, the phone was ringing. It was Dad. I didn't tell him about my **ordeal**(历险); I didn't want to worry him.

"Oh, I forgot to tell you!" he said. "I had an extra car key made and slipped it into your pocketbook—just in case you ever need it."

Today, I keep that key in my dresser drawer and treasure it. Whenever I hold it in my hand, I am reminded of all the wonderful things Dad has done for me over the years. I realize that, although he is now 68 and I am 40, I still look to him for wisdom, guidance and reassurance. Most of all, I **marvel**(惊奇) at the fact that his thoughtful gesture of making the extra key may have saved my life. And I understand how a simple act of love can make extraordinary things happen.

75

My Highest Compliment

It seems to me that all writers, including those who deserve to be classified as geniuses, need encouragement, particularly in their early years. I always knew I could write, but that just meant I wrote a little better than the other kids in my classes. That I might one day write well enough to **derive**(得到) income from my efforts, oddly enough, never occurred to me during my grade school and high school years.

There was a particular teacher at Hyde Park High School in Chicago, Illinois, who, simply by concentrating her attention on me, made me believe that I might be able to master the **knack**(才能) of writing well enough to consider the craft as a profession. Her name was Marguerite Byrne, and she taught English, which, of course, involved writing skills. Whatever instruction she shared with me was exactly the same as all her other students enjoyed, but the difference was that she encouraged me to begin the process of **submitting**(投稿) things I was writing, in that day, chiefly poems.

To my surprise the *Chicago Tribune*(《芝加哥论坛报》) not only thought enough of several of my verses to publish them, but also paid me—**inadvertently**(非故意地), the highest compliment a **fledgling**

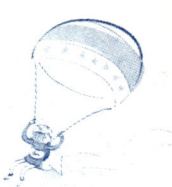

（初出茅庐的）author can receive. The editor wrote a confidential letter to Miss Byrne, asking her to see, if by chance, one of her students—a certain Stephen Allen, might be guilty of **plagiarism**（剽窃）. The editor's suspicions had been roused because, he was kind enough to say, he found it hard to believe that a seventeen-year-old could create material on such a professional level.

When Miss Byrne shared the letter with me, I was ecstatic! It was wonderfully encouraging. Maybe I really am a writer, I thought.

Miss Byrne also encouraged me to enter a contest **sponsored**（主办）by the CIVITAN organization. The assignment was to write an essay titled "Rediscovering America". Some days later, I was literally astonished when I received a letter saying that I was the winner of the contest. The prize was a check for one-hundred dollars and an invitation to an **all-the-trimmings banquet**（盛宴）at a hotel in downtown Chicago.

My mother, at the time, was not even aware that I was interested in writing, or if she had somehow found out about it, she took little notice. When I arrived back home that evening, she didn't ask how the evening had gone. I placed the one-hundred dollars on the breakfast table where she would see it when she awoke in the morning. Then I went immediately to bed.

This **scenario**（情景）demonstrates the tremendous importance of giving young people caring attention and encouraging them to develop and practice such gifts as they might have. Years later, I was able to repay my debt to Marguerite Byrne by **dedicating**（奉献）one of my books, *Wry on the Rocks* —A Collection of Poems, to her.

On the other hand, without encouragement talented students may never be motivated to learn, develop skills, or reach their full potential. For example, at the same high school, there was a teacher whose Spanish language classes I attended but from whom I, unfortunately learned very little simply because of the woman's cold sarcastically critical attitude. She seemed to know nothing about encouraging students, and she was gifted speaking **contemptuously**

(鄙视地) of those of us who weren't learning fast enough. Her negativism drove me away. Partly because of this teacher's negative influence, I am not fluent in Spanish today.

You see, I had already learned that one can derive instructive benefit from bad examples—by avoiding that behavior. **Alcoholism**(酗酒) was a serious problem in my mother's family. As a result of having seen enough examples of alcoholic excess in my childhood, I have never had any interest in drinking. The same applies to smoking. My poor mother was a two-pack a day victim of **nicotine addiction**(尼古丁成瘾), and because of the endless clouds of smoke, the coughing, the overfilled **ashtrays**(烟灰缸), and the ugly smell of cigarette smoke in the house and in my clothing, I have never smoked a cigarette in my life.

Again, young writers need to be encouraged. Because of Miss Byrne's influence, I have enjoyed a lifetime writing books, songs, and TV **scripts**(剧本). And guess what? I haven't plagiarized a single word of any of it.

76

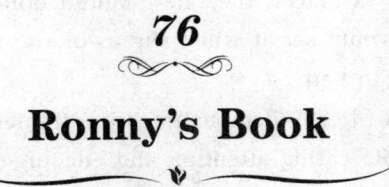

Ronny's Book

At first glance, Ronny looked like every other kid in the first-grade classroom where I **volunteered as**(自愿担任) the Reading Mom. Wind-blown hair, **scuffed**(磨损的) shoes, a little bit of dirt behind his ears, some kind of sandwich **smear**(污迹) around his mouth.

On closer inspection, though, the layer of dirt on Ronny's face, the crusty nose, and the packed **grime**(污垢) under his fingernails told me he didn't get dirty at school. He arrived that way.

His clothes were **ragged**(褴褛) and mismatched, his shoes had

string for laces, and his backpack was no more than a plastic shopping bag.

Along with his outward appearance, Ronny stood apart from his classmates in other ways, too. He had a **speech impediment**(语言障碍), wasn't reading or writing at grade-level, and had already been held back a year, making him eight-year-old in the first grade. His home life was a **shambles**(一团糟) with transient parents who uprooted him at their whim. He had yet to live a full year in any one place.

I quickly learned that beneath his **grungy exterior**(肮脏的外表), Ronny possessed a spark, a **resilience**(韧劲) that I'd never seen in a child who faced such tremendous odds.

I worked with all the students in Ronny's class on a one-on-one basis to improve their reading skills. Each day, Ronny's head twisted around as I came into the classroom, and his eyes followed me as I set up in a corner, **imploring**(乞求), "Pick me! Pick me!" Of course I couldn't pick him every day. Other kids needed my help, too.

On the days when it was Ronny's turn, I'd give him a silent nod, and he'd fly out of his chair and bound across the room in a blink. He sat awfully close—too close for me in the beginning, I must admit, and opened the book we were **tackling**(抓着) as if he were unearthing a treasure the world had never seen.

I watched his dirt-caked fingers move slowly under each letter as he struggled to sound out "Bud the Sub." It sounded more like "Baw Daw Saw" when he said it because of his speech impediment and his difficulty with the alphabet.

Each word offered a challenge and a triumph wrapped as one; Ronny painstakingly sounded out each letter, then tried to put them together to form a word. Regardless of "ball" ended up as Bah-lah or "bow," the biggest grin would spread across his face, and his eyes would twinkle and overflow with pride. It broke my heart each and every time. I just wanted to **whisk him out of his life**(带他摆脱他的生活), take him home, clean him up and love him.

167

Many nights, after I'd tucked my own children into bed, I'd sit and think about Ronny. Where was he? Was he safe? Was he reading a book by flashlight under the blankets? Did he even have blankets?

The year passed quickly and Ronny had made some progress but hardly enough to bring him up to grade level. He was the only one who didn't know that, though. As far as he knew, he read just fine.

A few weeks before the school year ended, I held an awards ceremony. I had treats, gifts and **certificates of achievement**(奖状) for everyone: Best Sounder-Outer, Most Expressive, Loudest Reader, Fastest Page-Turner.

It took me a while to figure out where Ronny fit; I needed something positive, but there wasn't really much. I finally decided on "Most Improved Reader"—quite a stretch, but I thought it would do him a world of good to hear.

I presented Ronny with his certificate and a book—one of those Little Golden Books that cost forty-nine cents at the grocery store checkout. Tears rolled down his cheeks, streaking the ever-permanent layer of dirt as he clutched the book to his chest and floated back to his seat. I choked back the lump that rose in my throat.

I stayed with the class for most of the day; Ronny never let go of the book, not once. It never left his hands.

A few days later, I returned to the school to visit. I noticed Ronny on a bench near the playground, the book open in his lap. I could see his lips move as he read to himself.

His teacher appeared beside me. "He hasn't put that book down since you gave it to him. He wears it like a shirt, close to his heart. Did you know that's the first book he's ever actually owned?"

Fighting back tears, I approached Ronny and watched over his shoulder as his grimy finger moved slowly across the page. I placed my hand on his shoulder and asked, "Will you read me your book, Ronny?" He glanced up, **squinted**(眯眼看) into the sun, and moved over on the bench to make room for me.

And then, for the next few minutes, he read to me with more

expression, clarity, and ease than I'd ever thought possible from him. The pages were already dog-eared, like the book had been read thousands of times already.

When he finished reading, Ronny closed his book, stroked the cover with his grubby hand and said with great satisfaction, "Good book."

A quiet pride settled over us as we sat on that play-ground bench, Ronny's hand now was in mine. I at once wept and marveled at the young boy beside me. What a powerful **contribution**(贡献) the author of that *Little Golden Book* had made in the life of a disadvantaged child.

At that moment, I knew I would get serious about my own writing career and do what that author had done, and probably still does—care enough to write a story that changes a child's life, care enough to make a difference.

I **strive**(奋斗) to be that author.

Writers in Prison

I was doing a guest writing **workshop**(讲习班) at Susanville State Prison near the Sierra Nevada foothills in northern California. Most of the men **doing time**(服刑) there are sentenced to prison because of drugs. They are housed in huge dormitories in **bunk**(双层) beds. They have no privacy, no place to be alone, no place to think quietly. I had great apprehensions when I walked onto the prison grounds. I had taught writing workshops at many California prisons, but those prisons had **cells**(小牢房). In cells, even if they are shared with another **inmate**(囚犯), one can find at least a little writing time. Surely the

men here at Susanville were not going to be interested in what I had to offer.

I had decided to spend my two days giving a **monologue**(独白) workshop. I wanted the men to have a chance to write and then perform before a camera. I wanted them to see themselves on video before I left the prison at the end of the second day. I felt that life in this prison had probably **stripped**(剥夺) them of most of their identity and that writing and performance art might restore some sense of who they were or who they could be.

I was pleased that twenty men had signed up for the class. This was the **maximum**(最大) number I had said I could take. I spent the first hour with them, talking about what it was like to be a writer. Telling them that there was a joy and a freedom in the words. That no matter how much they were all forced to be alike, dress alike, eat the same food, keep the same hours, that in their writing they could finally be different. As different as they wanted to be. Writing, I told them, could be the most **liberating**(自由的) of all the arts. You can be free with the word. There are no limits. I told them that every time I picked up a pencil or sat down at a computer or a typewriter that it was as if I was coming home, coming home to my art, my words, that this was a world that no one else could take away. This art would sustain me throughout all my days.

The men listened well and when I finally had them start their writing projects, they worked hard. There was only one, a young, very handsome blond man, who I worried about. He was **reluctant**(不情愿) to share during that first day when I had them writing their monologues. Every other student read and rewrote and read again, but this man sat quietly, erasing, writing, tearing up drafts, starting again. Whenever I would approach his desk, he quietly covered his paper with his arms.

"Can I see?" I ask.

"It would be easier for me if you didn't," he would answer, and then a shy smile would appear.

I wondered what he was writing about. Even if he didn't share his writing with the class, he was writing. He was choosing to spend his whole day in this hot **stuffy**(闷的) classroom working on something called monologue. That morning he probably didn't even know the meaning of the word. This should make me happy. But it didn't. I was concerned about his need for privacy, about his inability to share, knowing that he didn't think his writing was good enough.

I had worked in prisons for too many years to be fooled by his shyness. I knew that many of the inmates had learned at a very young age that they could do nothing right. They had been **abused**(虐待) and **tormented**(折磨) as children and lacked any self-confidence. But no matter how much I praised the other prisoners, he wouldn't **relent**(变温和). He went back to his dormitory that evening with his writing tucked into his jeans pocket. Many of the other men just left their work on the desks. Not him. He was taking no chance that I would read it after he was locked away behind the bars. He was right, of course. I would have **made a beeline** right **for**(径直走向) his desk the minute he got out the door. He had judged me right.

The second day all the men returned to the classroom. This was particularly pleasing to me. Even the young blond man. This was the day for reading and taping. I wondered how the silent, shy student would handle this. I was actually surprised to see him there. He had combed his long, blond hair and his shirt was neatly pressed. He had obviously thought about the fact that he was going to be filmed and wanted to look his best. At last I was going to hear what he wrote.

He didn't say much during the performances. I had given the men fairly loose instructions about who should be speaking in their monologues. I had, though, told them that I wanted to hear their characters tell me what it was they really wanted, what it was that no one understood about them, and why they needed to talk. He sat there quietly, watching the work of his fellow inmates. One of the men had written a monologue for God, and another had been Abraham Lincoln, another Martin Luther King. Some of the monologues were funny, others serious. Even though they hadn't had time to memorize their lines, once they began reading, the scripts in their hands were hardly noticeable, and I was extremely moved by their work.

Finally, he was the only one who hadn't read his monologue. When all the others were finished, I asked him, "Are you ready now?"

"I don't think so," he answered in such a gentle voice. Then the men were on him.

"Man, if I can do it, you can do it. Try it. You'll like it. Come on, man, don't be shy. Nobody's going to judge you here."

So he got up, took his script to the performance area and stood before the camera. He looked so young. The papers in his hands were shaking like frightened birds, but he looked with determination into the eye of the camera and opened up his monologue.

"My name is Bruce. I am twenty-one years old and I am dead. I am dead because I spent time in prison for drugs and I didn't care. I didn't care about me. I went to bed every night just counting the days 'till I could get out and get that next **fix**(困境). I would kill for my next fix. I would kill for my next fix."

He went on about his life, how he was raised in poverty by alcoholic parents, beaten, hungry, no life at all, shuffled back and forth through **foster homes**(抚养孤儿的家庭). While he read, he showed **scars**(伤疤)on his body, the burn marks on his arms where a drunken father had **extinguished**(弄熄) cigarettes, the cuts on his **wrists**(手腕) where he had tried to take his own life. I couldn't help it. The tears began forming in my eyes, hot and painful. My God, why had I asked him to share this horrible pain? Then he got to the end of his story.

"Even though I died right there in prison, I want to tell you something. The reason I need to talk to you today. I have risen again, just like in the *Bible*. I am reborn. One day a woman came in and told me to write. And I had never written before, but I did it anyway. I sat for eight hours in a chair and **focused**(专心) the way I have never focused before. I could never even sit still before! I wrote out my ugly

life, and then I was able to finally feel something, to feel pity for myself, when no one else was ever able to feel it. And I felt something else. I felt joy. I was writing, and what I was writing was good. I was a writer! And I was going to get up in front of all those men in that class, and I would say that this…"

At these words he held up his little manuscript. "This is more important to me than any drug. What I wanted to tell you was that I died a drug addict, and I was reborn as a writer."

We all sat there stunned. The camera kept running. He took a self-conscious little bow. Then he said, "Thank you," once again in his quiet voice. And then the men broke out in spontaneous applause. He walked over to me and took my hands. Inmates are not allowed to touch their teachers, but I let him anyway.

"You have given me something," he said, "that no drug has ever given me. My self-respect."

I think of him often. I pray that he has continued to find respect for himself through the written words. I know, though, that that day in that room with those men, a writer was born. After a long and terrible journey, a lost soul had come home, home to the words.

78

Coffee Shop Kindness

My senior year of high school was an extremely busy one, to say the least. If I wasn't studying and worrying about my grades, I was **juggling**(耍弄) many kinds of **extracurricular**(学校课程以外的) activities or attempting to make sense of my plans for college. It seemed as if my life had turned into one crazy cloud of confusion and I was **stumbling**(绊脚) around blindly, hoping to find some sort of

173

direction.

Finally, as senior year began to wind down, I got a part-time job working at the local coffee shop. I had figured that the job would be easy and, for the most part, stress-free. I pictured myself pouring the best **gourmet**(美味) coffees, making delicious **doughnuts**(炸面包圈), and becoming close friends with the regular customers.

What I hadn't **counted on**(期待) were the people with enormous orders who chose to use the drive-through window, or the women who felt that the coffee was much too creamy, or the men who wanted their iced coffees remade again and again until they reached a certain level of perfection. There were moments when I was **exasperated**(激怒) with the human race as a whole, simply because I couldn't seem to please anyone. There was always too much sugar, too little ice, and not enough **skim milk**(脱脂乳). Nevertheless, I kept at it.

One miserable rainy day, one of my regular customers came in looking depressed and defeated. My co-worker and I asked what the problem was and if we could help, but the customer wouldn't reveal any details. He just said he felt like crawling into bed, pulling the sheets up over his head, and staying there for a few years. I knew exactly how he felt.

Before he left, I handed him a bag along with his iced coffee. He looked at me questioningly because he hadn't ordered anything but the coffee. He opened the bag and saw that I had given him his favorite type of doughnut.

"It's **on me**(我请客)," I told him. "Have a nice day."

He smiled and thanked me before turning around and heading back out into the rain.

The next day was a horrible one. The rain was still spilling down from the sky in huge buckets and everyone in my town seemed to be using the drive-through window because no one wanted to brave the black skies or the thunder and lightning.

I spent my afternoon hanging out the window, handing people their orders and waiting as they slowly counted their pennies. I tried to

smile as the customers complained about the weather, but it was difficult to smile as they sat in their temperature-controlled cars with the windows rolled up, while I dealt with huge **droplets**(滴) of water hanging from my **visor**(舌帽), a shirt that was thoroughly **soaked**(湿透) around the collar, and an air conditioner that blasted out cold air despite the fact that it was only sixty-seven degrees outside. On top of that, no one felt like tipping that day. Every time I looked into our tip jar, with its small amount of pennies, I grew more depressed.

Around seven o'clock that evening, however, my day took a turn for the better. I was in the middle of making another pot of vanilla **hazelnut**(榛实) coffee when the customer from the day before drove up to the window. But instead of ordering anything, he handed me a single pink rose and a little note. He said that not too many people take the time to care about others and he was glad there were still people like me in the world. I was speechless and very touched; I hadn't thought that I had done anything incredible. After a moment, I came to my senses and thanked him. He told me I was welcome and with a friendly wave he drove away.

I waited until I saw his jeep exit the parking lot, then I ran to the back of the shop and read the note. It read:

"Christine,

Thanks for being so sweet, kind and thoughtful yesterday. I was sincerely touched by you. It is so nice to meet someone that's genuinely nice, warm and sensitive and unselfish. Please don't change your ways because I truly believe that you will excel.

Have a great day!

Hank"

As time went on, I did come across more complaining customers. But anytime I felt depressed or just plain sick of coffee, I thought of Hank and his kindness. Then I would smile, hold my head up high, clear my throat and ask politely, "How can I help you?"

79

The Giving Trees

I was a single parent of four small children, working at a minimum-wage job. Money was always tight, but we had a roof over our heads, food on the table, clothes on our backs, and if not a lot, always enough. My kids told me that in those days they didn't know we were poor. They just thought Mom was cheap. I've always been glad about that.

It was Christmas time, and although there wasn't money for a lot of gifts, we planned to celebrate with church and family, parties and friends, drives downtown to see the Christmas lights, special dinners, and by decorating our home.

But the big excitement for the kids was the fun of Christmas shopping at the mall. They talked and planned for weeks ahead of time, asking each other and their grandparents what they wanted for Christmas. I **dreaded**(担心) it. I had saved $120 for presents to be shared by all five of us.

The big day arrived and we started out early. I gave each of the four kids a twenty dollar bill and reminded them to look for gifts about four dollars each. Then everyone scattered. We had two hours to shop;

then we would meet back at the "Santa's workshop" display.

Back in the car driving home, everyone was in high Christmas spirits, laughing and teasing each other with hints and clues about what they had bought. My younger daughter, Ginger, who was about eight years old, was unusually quiet. I noted she had only one small, flat bag with her after her shopping **spree**(狂欢). I could see enough through the plastic bag to tell that she had bought candy bars—fifty-cent candy bars! I was so angry. What did you do with that twenty dollar bill I gave you? I wanted to yell at her, but I didn't say anything until we got home. I called her into my bedroom and closed the door, ready to be angry again when I asked her what she had done with the money. This is what she told me:

"I was looking around, thinking of what to buy, and I stopped to read the little cards on one of the Salvation Army's 'Giving Trees'. One of the cards was for a little girl, four years old, and all she wanted for Christmas was a doll with clothes and a hairbrush. So I took the card off the tree and bought the doll and hairbrush for her and took it to the Salvation Army **booth**(货棚).

"I only had enough money left to buy candy bars for us," Ginger continued. "But we have so much and she doesn't have anything."

I never felt so rich as I did that day.

80

The Last Straw

It was another long, winter afternoon with everyone stuck in the house and the four children were at it again— **bickering**(争吵), teasing, fighting over their toys. At times like these, Mother was almost ready to believe that her children didn't love each other, though

she knew that wasn't really true. All brothers and sisters fight, of course, but lately her little lively bunch had been particularly horrible to each other, especially Eric and Kelly, who were just a year apart. They seemed determined to spend the whole winter making each other miserable.

"Give me that. It's mine!"

"Is not, **fatso**(胖子)! I had it first!"

Mother sighed as she listened to the latest argument coming from the living room. With Christmas only a month away, the house seemed sadly lacking in Christmas spirit. This was supposed to be the season of sharing and love, of warm feelings and happy hearts. A home needed more than just pretty packages or twinkling lights on the tree to fill it with the Christmas spirit. But how could any mother **convince**(使明白) her children that being kind to each other was the most important way to get ready for Christmas.

Mother had only one idea. Years ago her grandmother had told her about an old Christmas custom that helped people discover the real meaning of Christmas. Perhaps it would work for her family. It was worth a try. Mother gathered her four little **rascals**(淘气鬼) together and sat them down on the stairs, smallest to tallest—Mike, Randi, Kelly and Eric.

"How would you kids like to start a new Christmas project this year?" she asked. "It's like a game, but it can only be played by people who can keep a secret. Can everyone here do that?"

"I can!" shouted Eric, wildly waving his arm in the air.

"I can keep a secret better than he can," yelled Kelly, jumping up and waving her arm in the air, too. If this was a contest, she wanted to make sure she beat Eric.

"I can do it!" **chimed in**(插话) Randi, not quite sure what was happening but not wanting to be left out.

"Me too, me too, me too," **squealed**(尖叫) little Mike, bouncing up and down.

"Well then, here's how the game works," Mother explained.

178

"This year we're going to surprise Baby Jesus when he comes on Christmas eve by making him the softest bed in the world. We're going to build a little **crib**(小儿床) for him to sleep in right here in our house, and we'll fill it with straw to make it comfortable. But here's the **catch**(难题): Each piece of straw we put in the crib will represent one kind thing we do for someone between now and Christmas. The more kind things we do, the more straw there will be for Baby Jesus. The secret part is—we can't tell anyone what good things we're doing and who we're doing them for."

The children looked confused. "How will Baby Jesus know it's his bed?" asked Kelly.

"He'll know," said Mother. "He'll recognize it by the love we've put into the crib, by how soft it is."

"But who will we do the kind things for?" asked Eric.

"It's simple," said Mother. "We'll do them for each other. Once every week between now and Christmas, we'll put all of our names in this hat, mine and Daddy's too. Then we'll each draw a name and do kind things for that person for a whole week. But here's the hard part. We can't tell anyone whose name we've drawn for that week, and we'll each try to do as many favors as we can for our special person without getting caught. And for every secret good thing we do, we'll put another piece of straw in the crib."

"But what if I pick someone I don't like?" frowned Kelly.

Mother thought about that for a minute. "Maybe you could use extra fat straws for the good things you do for that person, because they might be harder to do. But just think how much faster the fat straws will fill up our crib. Then on Christmas eve we'll put Baby Jesus in his little bed, and he'll sleep that night on a **mattress**(床垫) made of love. I think he'd like that, don't you?"

"Now, who will build the crib for us?" she asked.

Since Eric was the oldest, and the only one of the children allowed to use tools, he marched off to the basement to give it a try. For the next couple of hours loud banging and sawing noises came from the

basement. Then for a long time there were no noises at all. Finally Eric climbed back up the stairs with the crib in his arms.

"Here it is," he grinned. "The best crib in the world! And I did it all myself."

For once, everyone agreed: the little crib was the best in the world. One leg was an inch too short, of course, and the crib rocked a bit. But it had been built with love—and about a hundred bent nails, and it would certainly last a long time.

"Now we need some straw," said Mother, and together they headed out to the car to go searching for some in the nearby fields. Surprisingly, no one fought over who was going to sit in the front seat that day as they drove around the countryside, looking for an empty field. At last they saw a small patch of land that had been covered with tall grass in summer. Now, in mid-December, the grass had dried down to yellow **stalks**(茎, 秆) that looked just like real straw.

Mother stopped the car and the kids scrambled out to pick handfuls of the long grass.

"That's enough!" Mother finally laughed, when she saw that the cardboard box in the trunk was almost overflowing. "Remember, it's only a small crib."

So home they went, where they spread the straw carefully on a tray Mother had put on the kitchen table. The empty crib was placed gently on top, and the straw hid its one short leg.

"When can we pick names?" shouted the children.

"As soon as Daddy comes home for dinner," Mother answered.

At the supper table that night, the six names were written on separate pieces of paper, **folded up**(折叠) and shuffled around in an old baseball hat. Then the drawing began.

Kelly picked first and immediately started to giggle. Randi reached into the hat next. Daddy glanced at his scrap of paper and smiled quietly behind his hand. Mother picked out a name, but her face never gave away a clue. Next, little Mike reached into the hat, but since he couldn't read yet, Daddy had to whisper in his ear and tell him which

name he had picked. Eric was the last to choose, and as he unfolded his piece of paper, a frown crossed his face. But he put the name in his pocket and said nothing. The family was ready to begin.

The week that followed was filled with surprises. It seemed the house had suddenly been **invaded**(入侵) by an army of invisible **elves**（精灵）, and good things were happening everywhere. Kelly would walk into her room at bedtime and find her little blue nightgown neatly **laid out**(折整齐) and her bed turned down. Someone cleaned up the **sawdust**(锯末) under the workbench without being asked. The jelly **blobs**（斑点） disappeared magically from the kitchen counter after lunch one day while Mother was getting the mail. And every morning, while Eric was brushing his teeth, someone crept quietly into his room and made his bed. It wasn't made perfectly, but it was made.

"Where are my shoes?" asked Daddy one morning. No one seemed to know, but before he left for work, they were back in the closet, all shined up.

Mother noticed other changes during that week, too. The children weren't teasing or fighting as much. An argument would start and then suddenly stop for no good reason. Even Eric and Kelly seemed to be getting along better. In fact, all the children wore secret smiles and giggled to themselves at times.

By Sunday, everyone was anxious to pick new names again, and this time there was even more laughter and merriment during the picking process, except for Eric. Once again he unfolded his paper, looked at it, and put it in his pocket without a word. Mother noticed, but said nothing.

The second week of the game brought more amazing events. The garbage was taken out without anyone being asked. Someone even did two of Kelly's hard math problems one night when she left her homework out on the table.

The little pile of straw grew higher and softer. With only two weeks left until Christmas, the children wondered if their homemade bed would be comfortable enough for Baby Jesus.

"Who will be Baby Jesus anyway?" Randi asked on the third Sunday night after they had all picked new names.

"Perhaps we can use one of the dolls," said Mother. "Why don't you and Mike be in charge of picking out the right one?"

The two younger children ran off to gather up their favorite dolls, but everyone else wanted to help pick Baby Jesus, too. Little Mike dragged his Bozo the Clown rag doll from his room and proudly handed it over, sniffling later when everyone laughed. Soon Eric's well-hugged **teddy bear**(玩具熊), Bruffles, joined the dolls filling up the couch. Barbie and Ken were there, along with Kermit the Frog, stuffed dogs and lambs, and even a **cuddly**(可抱的) monkey that Grandma and Grandpa had sent Mike one year. But none of them seemed quite right.

Only an old baby doll, who had been loved almost to pieces, looked like a possibility for their Baby Jesus. "Chatty Baby," she had once been called, before she stopped chatting forever after too many baths.

"She looks so funny now," said Randi, and it was true. Once while playing beauty shop, Kelly had cut her own blonde hair along with Chatty Baby's, giving them both a **raggedly**(参差不齐的) **crew cut**(平头). Kelly's hair had eventually grown back, but Chatty Baby's never had. Now the wisps of blonde hair that stuck out all over the dolls head made her look a little lost and forgotten. But her eyes were still bright blue and she still had a smile on her face, even though her face was **smudged**(变脏)here and there by the touch of many **chubby**(胖乎乎) little fingers.

"I think she's perfect," said Mother. "Baby Jesus probably didn't have much hair when he was born either, and I bet he'd like to be represented by a doll who's had so many hugs."

So the decision was made and the children began to make a new **outfit**(服装) for their Baby Jesus—a little leather vest out of some **scraps**(废料) and some cloth diapers. Best of all, Baby Jesus fit perfectly into the little crib, but since it wasn't quite time for him to sleep there yet, he was laid carefully on a shelf in the hall closet to

wait for Christmas eve.

Meanwhile, the pile of straw grew and grew. Every day brought new and different surprises as the secret elves stepped up their activity. The home was finally filled with Christmas spirit. Only Eric had been unusually quiet since the third week of name picking.

The final night of name picking was also the night before Christmas eve. As the family sat around the table waiting for the last set of names to be put in the hat, Mother said, "You've all done a wonderful job. There must be hundreds of straws in our crib—maybe a thousand. You should be so pleased with the bed you've made. But remember, there's still one whole day left. We all have time to do a little more to make the bed even softer before tomorrow night. Let's try."

For the last time, the hat was passed around the table. Little Mike pulled out a name, and Daddy whispered it to him, just as he had done every week. Randi unfolded hers carefully under the table, peeked at it and hunched up her shoulders, smiling. Kelly reached into the hat and giggled happily when she saw the name. Mother and Daddy each took their turns, too, and then handed the hat with the last name to Eric. But as he unfolded the small scrap of paper and read it, his face **pinched up**(收缩) and he suddenly seemed about to cry. Without a word, he ran from the room.

Everyone immediately jumped up from the table, but Mother stopped them. "No, stay where you are," she said. "Let me talk to him alone first."

Just as she reached the top of the stairs, Eric's door banged open. He was trying to pull his coat on with one hand while he carried a small suitcase with the other hand.

"I have to leave," he said quietly, through his tears. "If I don't, I'll spoil Christmas for everyone!"

"But why? And where are you going?" asked Mother.

"I can sleep in my **snowbank**(雪堆) for a couple of days. I'll come home right after Christmas. I promise."

Mother started to say something about freezing and snow and no

183

mittens(手套) or boots, but Daddy, who was now standing just behind her, put his hand on her arm and shook his head. The front door closed, and together they watched from the window as the little boy with the sadly **slumped**(垂下的) shoulders and no hat **trudged**(吃力地走) across the street and sat down on a snowbank near the corner. It was very dark outside, and cold, and a few snow **flurries**(小雪) drifted down on the small boy and his suitcase.

"But he'll freeze!" said Mother.

"Give him a few minutes alone," said Dad quietly. "Then you can talk to him."

The little boy was already dusted with white when Mother walked across the street 10 minutes later and sat down beside him on the snowbank.

"What is it, Eric? You've been so good these last few weeks, but I know something's been bothering you since we first started the crib. Can you tell me, honey?"

"Aw, Mom, don't you see?" he sniffed. "I tried so hard, but I can't do it anymore, and now I'm going to spoil Christmas for everyone." With that he burst into sobs and threw himself into his mother's arms.

"But I don't understand," Mother said, brushing the tears from his face. "What can't you do? And how could you possibly spoil Christmas for us?"

"Mom," the little boy said through his tears, "you just don't understand. I got Kelly's name all four weeks! And I hate Kelly! I can't do one more nice thing for her or I'll die! I tried, Mom. I really did. I sneaked in her room every night and fixed her bed. I even laid out her dirty nightgown. I emptied her wastebasket, and I did some homework for her one night when she was going to the bathroom. Mom, I even let her use my race car one day, but she smashed it right into the wall like always!

"I tried to be nice to her, Mom. Even when she called me a stupid **dummy**(笨蛋) because the crib leg was short, I didn't hit her. And

every week, when we picked new names, I thought it would be over. But tonight, when I got her name again, I knew I couldn't do one more nice thing for her, Mom. I just can't! And tomorrow's Christmas eve. I'll spoil Christmas for everybody just when we're ready to put Baby Jesus in the crib. Don't you see why I had to leave?"

They sat together quietly for a few minutes, Mother's arm around the small boy's shoulders. Only an occasional **sniffle**(抽噎) and **hiccup** (打嗝) broke the silence on the snowbank.

Finally Mother began to speak softly, "Eric, I am so proud of you. Every good thing you did should count as double because it was especially hard for you to be nice to Kelly for so long. But you did all those nice things anyway, one straw at a time. You gave your love when it wasn't easy to give. Maybe that's what the spirit of Christmas is really all about. If it's too easy to give, maybe we're not really giving much of ourselves after all. The straws you added were probable the most important ones, and you should be proud of yourself.

"Now, how would you like a chance to earn a few easy straws like the rest of us? I still have the name I picked tonight in my pocket, and I haven't looked at it yet. Why don't we **switch**(交换), just for the last day? It will be our secret."

"That's not cheating?"

"It's not cheating," Mother smiled.

Together they dried the tears, brushed off the snow and walked back to the house.

The next day the whole family was busy cooking and straightening up the house for Christmas Day, wrapping last-minute presents and trying hard not to burst with excitement. But even with all the activity and eagerness, a flurry of new straws piled up in the crib, and by nightfall it was overflowing. At different times while passing by, each member of the family, big and small, would pause and look at the wonderful pile for a moment, then smile before going on. It was almost time for the tiny crib to be used. But was it soft enough? One straw might still make a difference.

For that very reason, just before bedtime, Mother tip-toed quietly to Kelly's room to lay out the little blue nightgown and turn down the bed. But she stopped in the doorway, surprised. Someone had already been there. The nightgown was laid neatly across the bed and a small red race car rested next to it on the pillow.

The last straw was Eric's after all.

81

Are You God?

One cold evening during the holiday season, a little boy about six or seven was standing out in front of a store window. The little child had no shoes on and his clothes were mere rags. A young woman passing by saw the little boy and could read the longing in his pale blue eyes. She took the child by the hand and led him into the store. There she bought him new shoes and a complete suit of warm clothing.

They came back outside into the street and the woman said to the child, "Now you can go home and have a very happy holiday."

The little boy looked up at her and asked, "are you God, Ma'am?"

She smiled down at him and replied, "No, son, I'm just one of His children."

The little boy then said, "I knew you had to be some relation(亲属) of God."

82

Timmy's Wish

It was under an old **Banyan**(榕树) tree on the school playground in Hawaii that I first met Timmy. I was an elementary school teacher and he was a **gregarious**(合群的) five-year-old. As the school year progressed, a special friendship between us began to evolve. It was the "Summer Fun Program" at our school that really brought us together.

One day in mid-August, I was in the school office when Timmy's teacher came running in with Timmy. He was sobbing and the teacher was nearly **hysterical**(歇斯底里的). The bathroom door had slammed on his finger. She had a handkerchief wrapped around Timmy's **index finger**(食指) and wasn't sure how much of it was left because it was bleeding so much. Our school bus driver rushed them immediately to the Emergency Room.

A few minutes later the phone rang at the school. It was the doctor asking if we had found the **tip**(末端) of Timmy's finger. He said there was a small chance of saving it if we could get it to him quickly. Pulling myself out of a **daze**(茫然), I ran to the bathroom. Sure enough, there it was. After carefully wrapping it up, I grabbed my car keys and headed for the emergency unit.

  The doctor was waiting for me. Unfortunately, the fingertip had already turned blue. As he took the tiny piece of flesh in his hand, I knew from the look on his face that it was too late. With a sinking heart I quietly asked, "Where's Timmy?"

  The doctor pointed to a room down the hall. "He's soaking his finger in a **solution**(溶液) to stop the bleeding."

  "Can I see him for a few minutes?" I asked.

  "Of course," he said and gestured toward the door.

  Timmy was lying on a bed. He must have been sobbing a lot because his chest was still **heaving**(起伏) as I approached the bed.

  "Hi, Timmy," I said, gently brushing the tears from his cheeks. "How are you doing?"

  "Okay," he whimpered, trying to hold back his tears.

  I felt helpless, unable to take the pain away from my little friend. Then suddenly, an idea came to me. Bending over, I whispered in his ear, "Timmy, did you know that our Hawaiian **lizards**(蜥蜴) grow their tails back and little boys can grow their fingers back too?"

  Timmy's soft green eyes grew wide with excitement. "They can?" he asked, obviously astonished by the thought.

  "Yes, they can!" I answered with certainty.

  "How?" he asked.

  "Close your eyes and I'll show you."

  I wanted to teach him the ancient Hawaiian methods of visual **imagery**(意象) and **affirmations**(肯定) that I had learned in my youth. I had studied this process under the **tutelage**(指导) of special kupunas, or elders. My family has lived in the Hawaiian Islands for five generations. As we enter this new century, I find it encouraging that researchers at major universities are now **validating**(证实) this ancient wisdom. William A. Tiller, **Professor Emeritus**(荣誉教授), of Stanford University has said, "Many people still find it difficult to understand how the invisible energy of a wish can change the way the world works. However, extensive research already exists on the demonstrable effects of our wishes."

As Timmy closed his eyes, I began, "Good. Now Timmy, inside your head you have a little voice. Do you know the voice I am talking about?"

"Uh-huh," Timmy nodded, his eyes still closed tightly.

"With that voice inside your head, tell your finger how much you love it and how much you need it."

I could see Timmy's little face focused in deep **concentration**(专注).

"Tell your finger that you need it to dial the phone," I paused, watching his little lips silently repeat my words. "And to write your sentences in school." I paused again so he could say the words after me.

"And tell it how much you need it to point at things," I waited for another moment and then continued. "Now just say, grow for me finger, grow. I love you and I need you."

After a few moments, Timmy opened his eyes.

"How was that?" I asked.

Timmy's tear-stained face glowed. I continued, "Remember to do this every time you think of it during the day and wish your finger well."

Kissing him on the forehead, I said my goodbyes and started toward the door. Then I suddenly realized something. If the adults in his life are not aware of the real power of this technique, they might discourage him. Not wanting limiting beliefs to swallow up Timmy's possibilities for a miracle, I spun around and returned to his bedside.

"Timmy," I told him, "your finger is going to be perfectly fine. Let's wait until it's completely healed before we tell anybody about this special technique."

"Okay," he replied.

A few days later, Timmy arrived back in school with a large bandage on his finger. With a big grin on his face, he walked up to me and said quietly, "I'm talking to my finger every day, wishing it well, and it's listening to me."

Weeks later, with a joyful burst of energy, Timmy **sprinted**(疾跑) towards me. He proudly pulled the bandage off to show me the result of "his work".

"See," he said, "it's growing back really good!"

A year later, Timmy came to say goodbye to me. He and his family were moving to another neighborhood. Timmy's finger was completely healed. It was round and padded just as any index finger should be. Only a fine hairline scar remained.

Timmy remains forever in my heart as a constant reminder of the possibility of miracles. From him, I have learned to challenge the thought of failure as it comes into my mind. To this day, Timmy inspires me to reach beyond the accepted knowledge of the times, and to remember the kupuna wisdom that teaches all things are possible if you truly believe.

83

Win One for Me, Daddy

The 1987 season was a tough year. Up to that point, I was at the top of the world of racing. I had won three NASCAR Winston Cup **championships**(锦标赛). I had won about seventy races in NASCAR Winston Cup. Racing had been very good to me.

But in 1987, I was with a new team, and things weren't going very well. We were the dream team. I had the best backing from the Hendrick Motorsports Group, an excellent sponsorship, and the best engine builder in racing. However, going into the last part of the season, we still had not won a race. This had not happened to me since I got my first NASCAR Winston Cup win in 1975.

In addition to my not winning races, we found out that Stevie, my

wife, was pregnant. All of this was emotionally tough for me. Stevie had three **miscarriages**(流产) previously, including one in 1986. She had never been able to carry a baby to full term, and I felt badly for her. I leaned on her so much. She is my best friend and had always been with me at every race.

Now she was not able to go to the track each weekend with me. That was difficult. Stevie has always been such a part of my life and my racing career. We had always gone to races together. I had not experienced life at the track without Stevie. I have been deeply in love with her since we met in high school back in Owensboro, Kentucky. She had stood by me with much encouragement through the ups and downs and **boos**(嘘声) and cheers of fans. She had set a new standard in racing by being a part of my race team on Sundays at a time when women were not allowed in the **pits**(赛场). It was tough on me to be racing without her there.

On September 17, we were blessed with our first child, Jessica Leigh. We were very excited! I had to leave to go on to the next race later that week. The race was at Martinsville, Virginia, where I had won several times before. But I had no expectations of winning this time. As the race progressed, I really had no hope of winning, as I was a **lap**(跑道的一圈) down with just twenty-five laps to go. Dale Earnhardt was leading. When he stopped for fuel, I got back on the lead lap.

Then a caution came out with about seven laps to go. On the restart, I was in third place behind Earnhardt and Terry Labonte. Both of these guys were previous champions and were tough, hard racers. There was no way I was going to get by them with just a few laps to go. They could make it very difficult to get around them. On the final lap in the final turns of 3 and 4, Terry had gotten up beside Dale and left just a little opening for me to pass both of them, beating them to the finish line.

I won my first race of the year! It was much more special, though, than just being my first win of the season and my first victory with the

new team. For earlier that Sunday morning, appearing from nowhere, I was surprised to find a little rosebud in the seat of my car with a note that said, "Win one for me, Daddy!"

My first race of the season was sweetened by it occurring on the same day that I was first called "Daddy".

84

A Surprise Gift for Mother

On Christmas Day, all the joys of a close family relationship **radiated**(散发) throughout our parents' home. The smells of roasted turkey, Southern-baked ham and homemade bread hung in the air. Tables and chairs were set up everywhere to accommodate **toddlers** (学步孩童), teenagers, parents and grandparents. Every room was lavishly decorated. No family member had ever missed Christmas Day with our mother and father.

Only this year, things were different. Our father had passed away on November 26, and this was our first Christmas without him. Mother was doing her best to be the **gracious**(亲切的) hostess, but I could tell this was especially hard for her. I felt a catch in my throat, and again I wondered if I should give her my planned Christmas gift, or if it had become inappropriate in my father's absence.

A few months earlier I had been putting the finishing touches on portraits I had painted of each of my parents. I'd planned to give them as Christmas gifts. This would be a surprise for everyone, as I had not studied art or tried serious painting. There had been an undeniable **urge**(愿望) within that pushed me **relentlessly**(不懈地) to do this. The portraits did look like them, but I was still unsure of my painting techniques.

While painting one day, I was surprised by a doorbell ring. Quickly putting all my painting materials out of sight, I opened the door. To my astonishment, my father walked in alone, never before having visited me without my mother. Grinning, he said, "I've missed our early morning talks. You know, the ones we had before you decided to leave me for another man!" I hadn't been married long. Also, I was the only girl and the baby of the family.

Immediately I wanted to show him the paintings, but I was reluctant to ruin his Christmas surprise. Yet something urged me to share this moment with him. After **swearing**(使答应) him to secrecy, I insisted he keep his eyes closed until I had the portraits set on **easels**(画架).

"Okay, Daddy. Now you can look!"

He appeared **dazed**(惊奇的) but said nothing. Getting up, he walked closer to inspect them. Then he withdrew to eye them at a distance. Finally, with a tear escaping down one cheek, he mumbled, "I don't believe it. The eyes are so real that they follow you everywhere, and look how beautiful your mother is. Will you let me have them **framed**(装画框)?"

Thrilled(激动) with his response, I happily volunteered to drop them off the next day at the frame shop. Several weeks passed. Then one night in November the phone rang, and a cold chill numbed my body. I picked up the receiver to hear my husband, a doctor, say, "I'm in the emergency room. Your father has had a stroke. It's bad, but he is still alive."

Daddy lingered in a **coma**(昏迷) for several days. I went to see him in the hospital the day before he died. I slipped my hand in his and asked, "Do you know who I am, Daddy?"

He surprised everyone when he whispered, "You're my darling daughter."

He died the next day, and it seemed all joy was **drained**(离开) from the lives of my mother and me.

I finally remembered to call about the portrait framing and thanked

God my father had gotten a chance to see the pictures before he died. I was surprised when the shopkeeper told me my father had visited the shop, paid for the framing and had them gift-wrapped. In all our grief, I had no longer planned to give the portraits to my mother.

Even though we had lost the **patriarch**(家长) of our family, everyone was assembled on Christmas Day, making an effort to be cheerful. As I looked into my mother's sad eyes and unsmiling face, I decided to give her Daddy's and my gift. As she **stripped**(剥去) the paper from the box, I saw her heart wasn't in it. There was a small card inside attached to the pictures.

After looking at the portraits and reading the card, her entire **demeanor**(态度) changed. She bounced out of her chair, handed the card to me and told my brothers to hang the paintings facing each other over the fireplace. She stepped back and looked for a long while. With sparkling, tear-filled eyes and a wide smile, she quickly turned and said, "I knew Daddy would be with us on Christmas Day!"

I glanced at the gift card scrawled in my father's handwriting. "Mother, our daughter reminded me why I am so blessed. I'll be looking at you always. Daddy."

85

Christmas Presence

It was the night before Christmas, and all through the evening I **reminisced**(回忆往事), fondly reliving past Christmases spent with my family. As a second year nursing student, just nineteen, this was to be the first time I wouldn't be home on Christmas. Although I knew I would someday be working on Christmas, I never expected to feel this lonely.

  Secluded（躲进）in my room, I **yearned for**（渴望）the mouth-watering **aromas**（香味）of mom's freshly baked cookies, hot chocolate and love. The absence of the usual giggling, slamming doors and ringing telephones made the dormitory seem cold and empty. The unappetizing smell of **disinfectant**（消毒剂）replaced my visions of cookies and cocoa.

  Standing in front of the mirror, I **conversed**（交谈）with my reflection. "You wanted to be a nurse, didn't you? Well, you're almost a nurse. Now is your chance to find out what Christmas spirit really means."

  Determined to make the best of it, I turned in early.

  "I'll be home for Christmas. You can count on me..." My faithful clock-radio announced **reveille**（起床号）as I slowly dragged myself out of a toasty-warm bed. I trudged across the snow-filled street and grabbed a quick breakfast in the cafeteria before reporting for duty on the medical-surgical unit.

  As I prepared to take **vital signs**（健康状况）on my first patient, I was startled by a **robust**（强壮的）voice that came from behind. "Merry Christmas to you. Want anything from the cafeteria? I'm headed that way, Missy."

  As I took the **stethoscope**（听诊器）out of my ears and turned around, from the dimly lit room I could see a great, **roly-poly**（矮胖的）elderly gentleman with long, curly hair, all decked out in a bright red, plaid shirt tucked **haphazardly**（随意地）into baggy red trousers. The trousers appeared to be held up by only two, wide, fire-engine-red **suspenders**（吊裤带）that had long since outlived their **elasticity**（弹性）. This Santa Claus **facsimile**（仿真版）was standing in the doorway waiting patiently for an answer to his query. The only thing missing was the beard.

  As I looked toward the bright hallway lights from the darkened room, I thought for a moment that I was dreaming.

  "No, thanks," I responded. "I just came on duty. I'll grab something at lunch."

Before disappearing down the hall he added, "My name's George. Just let me know what I can do for you, Missy. I'll be right back."

As I cared for my patients, George was right alongside. I watched him spread holiday cheer as he became a guest to the patients who had no visitors that day. When trays arrived he knew who needed assistance and who needed to be fed. He read letters and cards to those whose eyes could no longer see the letters on a printed page. George's powerful body and tender hands were always ready to help hold, turn, pull-up or lift a patient. He was a "**gopher**"(地鼠) who made countless trips to the supply room for the "needs of the moment."

George also knew when to call for help. While reading a letter to Mr. Jenkins, George noticed that the patient suddenly started to "look funny" and at once ran to the nurse's station to summon aid. Thanks to George's swift action, we managed to **reverse**(防止) the effects of an **impending**(即将发生的) **diabetic coma**(糖尿病昏迷症).

George clearly enjoyed helping others while he spread cheer and told jokes—the same jokes, over and over again, all day long, one patient at a time. We all enjoyed his presence that Christmas day.

When I finally took my lunch break, I was surprised to find the cafeteria **elaborately**(精心地) decorated for the season. I sat down next to one of the staff nurses from the unit. During lunch with Andrea, I had the chance to ask a burning question. "Who is this George fellow? And why is he here on Christmas Day?"

"About ten years ago, George's wife became seriously ill. He spent almost every waking moment by her side. Those two lovebirds were so devoted to one another. There was nothing he wouldn't do for her." Andrea stopped for a few moments, sipping her coffee in silence, before continuing.

"George started to visit other patients while his wife was sleeping or having treatments. He was here so much that he seemed to take naturally to helping out wherever he could."

My natural curiosity made me ask, "Does he have any family?"

A serious look came over Andrea's face as she continued. "They

never had children, and as far as I know, there are no relatives. But you see, George watched his wife suffer for a very long time. He shared every second of her pain and **anguish**(折磨). On Christmas Eve night, after I prepared his wife for sleep, they prayed together. During the prayer, George promised his wife that if God would take away her misery that night, by taking her 'home,' he would spend the rest of his life as a Christmas volunteer."

Andrea and I finished our lunch in silence.

86

The Pillow

For twelve years, my church has participated in the Appalachia Service Project. One week each summer, volunteers travel to Kentucky, Tennessee, Virginia or West Virginia to repair or build homes for families.

At the age of sixteen, I went on my first volunteer project in West Virginia. On the night we arrived, we discovered that "our family" was living in a **trailer**(活动屋) that was in poor condition, no bigger than two parking spaces. A crew had been working on it for two weeks, but every time they finished one problem, another surfaced.

The staff soon decided that the only reasonable solution was to build a new house—something highly unusual but necessary under these circumstances. Normally the goal is to repair existing homes. "Our family" was overjoyed with their new house that was 20×30 foot with three bedrooms, a bath and a kitchen room.

On Tuesday of that week, while we all ate lunch together, I asked "our family's" three boys, Josh, Eric and Ryan, "What do you want for your new room?" **Anticipating**(预期) posters, toys and other

197

gadgets(小机械) that children usually ask for, we were surprised when Josh, the oldest, responded, "I just want a bed."

We were stunned. The boys had never slept in a bed. They were accustomed only to **foam pads**(泡沫垫). That night we had a meeting and unanimously decided that beds would be the perfect gift. On Thursday night, a few adults in our group drove to the nearest city and bought beds and new bedding. They arranged for everything to be delivered on Friday.

When Friday arrived, we could hardly contain ourselves. After lunch, when we saw the delivery truck coming, we told "our family" about the surprise. It was like watching ecstatic children on Christmas morning.

That afternoon, we set up the beds as we finished each room. Josh, who had his own room, wanted to put his bed together by himself. Eric and Ryan shared a room and got a new bunk bed. As we fitted the frames together, Eric, who had been working outside, ran into the house to watch us. Too dirty to enter his room, he observed with wide-eyed enthusiasm from the doorway.

As Meggan, a member of our group, slipped a pillowcase onto one of the pillows, Eric asked, "What is that?"

"A pillow," she replied.

"What do you do with it?" Eric persisted.

"When you go to sleep, you put your head on it," Meggan answered softly. Tears came to our eyes as she handed Eric the pillow.

"Oh...that's soft," he said, hugging it tightly.

Now, when my sister or I start to ask for something that seems urgent, my Dad gently asks, "Do you have a pillow?"

We know exactly what he means.

87

A Lot of Bread

When I was first **incarcerated**(监禁) in 1987, the hardest part of doing prison time was being away from my children. This is common with most of the women in prison, so often stories of our children are shared among each other.

Renee, a friend I had met in prison, was doing seven years for drug charges. She had a five-year-old son that her parents were raising. She and the grandparents had told the five-year-old that Renee was away at school in order to protect him from the fear and **humiliation**(耻辱) of his mother being incarcerated. Renee would call her son often and promise him that it wouldn't be long before they'd be reunited again.

One evening, after talking to her son, Renee came to me with tears in her eyes. Her son had asked if she would be home soon. Renee made the regular promise that it wouldn't be too much longer now. The boy asked, "Can we go to the **duck pond**(鸭池) to feed the ducks with bread when you get home?" She assured him that they would.

In the innocence of a child, he had proudly announced that he was saving up the bread already. Renee's heart **wrenched**(揪心疼) imagining the huge pile of moldy bread that would be piled up before

she would be able to keep her promise to this trusting five-year-old.

We cried together, and she somehow made it through the crisis. I was shocked when only a few weeks later she came to me seeking advice. She had just received her state pay—twenty-five dollars for the month, and had the opportunity to buy a half of a **pill**（毒品）for twenty-five dollars. It would leave her broke for the rest of the month, but Renee really wanted to buy the pill. It would be dissolved and shot up for a **high**（快感）. She felt that she deserved the "treat" because prison was so hard, she was so lonely and it was almost her birthday. I'm sure Renee had other reasons, but my head was still spinning from the fact that she could even consider it with a five-year-old son waiting to share her life with him.

Since I don't do drugs and never have, I couldn't imagine what kind of high could be greater than spending time with your child. Before I realized what I was saying, I blurted out, "You're grown, and you have to make your own decisions, but think how much bread that twenty-five dollars could buy."

The statement was like throwing ice water in Renee's face. She caught her breath, whirled around and walked away from me before I could take back my statement. I felt terrible. It was cruel of me to have made such a statement, I thought. Who was I to judge another person? I knew I had ruined a good friendship.

I didn't see Renee for several days, so I wasn't sure if she had used the state pay for the coveted half-pill. I felt miserable. Finally, Renee joined me at a table in the restroom, looking sheepish. I hugged her without asking about her decision—it was none of my business. She volunteered the information, anyway. Renee had not bought the pill.

She said, "You were right, Lucy. It will buy a lot of bread."

It's been ten years since I've seen Renee, but she still writes and lets me know that she still hasn't done drugs, although tempted. She always thinks about how much bread the cost of the drugs will buy. Renee and her son now visit the duck pond often. She continues to thank me for reminding her of what that one moment of weakness almost cost her.

88

Let Us Be United

September 10, 2001, was our eighth wedding anniversary. My husband, Alan, was leaving the next day for a week back in California to try his last Clean Water Act case. He'd decided to give up a thriving environmental law practice for a year's **sabbatical**(休假) spending more time with family and offering volunteer work in India. We spent the day celebrating our love for each other, planning our future and counting the blessings in our lives. We were so grateful for our life together. Alan always said, "When we wake up each morning, we should feel gratitude for being alive." And we did.

Alan woke up at 4:30 on Tuesday for his morning flight to San Francisco. As he kissed our five-year-old daughter Sonali and me goodbye, I pulled him toward me, knocking him over. He laughed heartily and said, "I'll return with the pot of gold."

"You are my pot of gold, Alan," I said. "Come home safe and sound."

He assured me he would, and at 7:00 a.m., he called to say he had checked in, he loved us, and he'd be back by the weekend.

And then it all began…The CNN announcer confirmed that Flight

93 bound for San Francisco had **crashed**（坠毁）in a field in Pennsylvania. In that instant, I felt a crushing blow. Devastated, with the wind knocked out of me, I could barely get a sound out as shock and disbelief poured through my veins. My heart literally stopped beating and I had to will myself to live. How could my husband, my best friend who I'd kissed goodbye hours earlier, be dead?

When Sonali came home from school, I let her play for an hour before I told her the news. I wanted to **savor**（享受）the innocence of her not knowing Daddy was dead. When she heard Alan's plane had crashed and he was not coming home, she **wailed**（哀号）a cry so deep and heartbreaking, a cry I pray I will never hear again from any living being. She sobbed for an hour straight, and then she looked me in the eyes and said, "I am so sad. But I'm not the saddest girl in the world. Some children have lost their Mommy and their Daddy, and I still have you."

A few days after the crash, Sonali's brother Chris, concerned that Sonali might not understand what was really happening, asked her, "Do you know where Daddy is?"

"Yes, he's at work!"

Chris was wondering how to handle this, when she continued. "Silly, he's in court of the heavens. Defending the angels."

Sonali's courage in the following weeks continue to amaze me and remind me of her Dad. One of Alan's final contemplations was a sentence he'd heard in a recent workshop, "Fear—Who Cares?" I know that these words helped guide him on September 11.

Sonali and I attended a memorial service at the crash site in Pennsylvania with her older brothers Chris and John. Standing at the fence, staring out at the field and the **scorched**（烧焦的）trees, I couldn't help but notice what a beautiful place it was for him to die. Such an expansive countryside with golden red trees—this is where it all ended for Alan.

Sonali picked up some dirt in her hands, folded her hands in prayer and began singing a beautiful **hymn**（圣歌）she learned in India

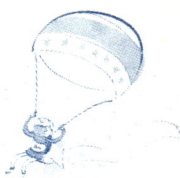

the previous winter. Everyone stopped to listen to her. Then she held the dirt to her heart and threw it toward the plane.

As the sun peeked momentarily through the thick cloud cover, Sonali looked up and said, "There's Daddy!" She drew a heart in the **gravel**(沙砾) and asked for some flowers, which she arranged beautifully around the heart with one flower in the center for her Daddy.

News of Sonali's courageous, sweet voice reached California, and we received a call from the governor's office. Would Sonali like to sing at California's Day of Remembrance?

"No, I don't think so. She just turned five a few weeks ago, and there will be too many people."

Sonali heard me and asked, "What am I too young to do?"

She listened to my reasons why not and simply said, "I want to do it."

I agreed.

And in the next few days, Sonali's **repertoire**(节目) of mostly Disney tunes expanded to include a beautiful prayer from the Rig Veda that we heard at the Siddha **Yoga Meditation Ashram**(瑜伽修行所) in New York where we were staying. Clearly, "Let Us Be United" was the perfect song for Sonali to sing:

Let us be united;

Let us speak in harmony;

Let our minds **apprehend**(理解) alike;

Common be our prayer;

Common be our **resolution**(决心);

Alike be our feeling;

Unified be our hearts;

Perfect be our unity.

On the flight back to California, our flight attendant heard about where we were going and asked if Sonali wanted to sing her song for everyone on the plane.

A bit concerned, my mother asked Sonali, "Do you know how many people are on this plane?"

Sonali had no idea. So she took the flight attendant's hand, walked up and down the aisle, and then came back with her guess.

"About a thousand," she said. "I can do that. I'll be fine."

In a clear, strong voice, Sonali sang to her fellow passengers. She then walked up and down the aisle with one of the crewmembers, receiving the smiles, thanks and love of all the United passengers. At the end of the flight, who stood on top of a box at the door with the flight attendant, thanking everyone and saying goodbye? Our Sonali!

When Sonali sang on the steps of the **state capitol**(议会大厦), her voice was unbelievably strong. It was as though she wanted to fill the whole universe with this impassioned prayer so it would reach her Daddy. As she sang, I felt it also become a pure prayer to everyone gathered—a prayer that painted a **vision**(梦想). I was delighted when she asked me if she could sing again, this time for Alan's memorial service at Grace Cathedral in San Francisco.

That wasn't Sonali's last singing prayer. When the Golden State Warriors awarded a check to the Beaven family at a **fundraiser**(募捐) in their honor, guess who sang to thousands of people in their stadium? When asked how she was able to sing in front of so many people, Sonali said, "I wasn't afraid because Daddy was singing with me."

October 15th would have been Alan's forty-ninth birthday, and Sonali wanted to have a birthday party for him. "Daddy's favorite place is the ocean, so let's go to the beach and have a big fire. Everybody can write a prayer on a piece of wood and when we put the wood in the fire, the prayers will rise to Daddy in heaven."

And so we did. As sweetly as Sonali's voice reached the heavens and so many hearts, so, too, our love rose into the moonlit sky. Alan's courage and spirituality are so strongly reflected in Sonali's ability to rise above her own heartbreak and loss and uplift people. Just as Alan didn't sit back in his seat with shaking knees but rose fearlessly to help save thousands of people's lives, so, too, Sonali chose not to bury herself in grief, but to sing her Dad's vision of love and courage. I am grateful for them both!

89

The Cat Lady

I have lived in my neighborhood for twenty years. It seems to me that I've spent at least ten of those years looking for a lost pet, either mine or one I'd seen listed in the newspaper's lost-pet column.

Recently, I was at it again, going door-to-door looking for one of my own lost kitties, a little black cat named Nicholas who'd slipped out the door before I could stop him. I made my rounds, visiting with all the neighbors, describing Nicholas. Familiar with this routine, everyone promised to keep an eye out and call me if they saw him.

Two blocks from my house, I noticed a gentleman cleaning the tree leaves in the yard of a home that had recently been sold. I introduced myself and presented my new neighbor with the **plight**(困境) of the missing Nicholas, asking if he had seen him.

"No," he replied, "I've not seen a little black kitty around here." He thought for a moment, looked at me and said, "But I know who you should ask. Several of my neighbors have told me that there's a woman in the neighborhood who's crazy about cats. They say she knows every cat around here, probably has dozens herself. They call her 'The Cat Lady.' Be sure to check with her."

205

"Oh, thank you," I said eagerly. "Do you know where she lives?"

He pointed a finger down the street, "It's that one."

I followed his finger and started to laugh.

He was pointing at my house!

90

For the Best

It was two days after the tragic school shooting in Colorado, and I was feeling bad about what had happened to the students there. My school began having a lot of bomb threats and it seemed that police cars were there often. I was standing with my friend, Amberly, and her boyfriend when he casually said, "I'm gonna **blow up**(炸平) the school and kill everyone."

I asked, "Why would you want to do that?"

He said, "I just do," and walked away.

I was scared because no one had ever said anything like that to me before. I found out when talking to other friends that he also **bragged about**(吹嘘) this to other people. My friends told me that I should tell an adult what he had said, but I was too scared and I made them promise not to tell anyone either.

One day, Amberly and I were talking about what he had said when the teacher overheard our conversation. She took me out into the hallway and made me tell her who had said it and what they had said. At first, I refused to say a word. She told me it really was for the best, so I told her. I felt awful for doing it. I was angry with her for making me tell who said it. I wasn't sure he really meant it and didn't want him to get into trouble.

He got **suspended**(被停学) for two days and had two days of in-

school **detention**(监禁) after that. I sometimes wonder if I had not told, would he have done what he said he was going to do? The guys in Colorado seemed pretty normal to a lot of people. The bottom line is, you should never joke around about something as serious as killing people. If you do, responsible people have no choice but to have you checked out to ensure everyone else's safety.

After he was suspended, the whole sixth grade had an assembly. The principal and counselors told the students that there was a kid who was making threats and that he was suspended. I decided later to tell him that it was me who told on him so he wouldn't **speculate**(思考) about who did it. I was surprised to find that he was not angry with me for doing what I did. He was able to get help for his feelings and behavior.

Many people are in the same situation that I was in. If your friend is saying threatening stuff like my friend was, then they obviously need help soon. It seems like when one school shooting happens, then another one occurs not too long after that. If there were any way that you could prevent one school shooting, it could perhaps save your own life and many others as well. If I had to do it over again, I would—because it really was for the best.

91

Albert

Working in a hospital with recent stroke patients was an **all-or-nothing**(孤注一掷的) job. They were usually going grateful to be alive or just wanted to die. A quick glance told all.

Albert taught me much about strokes.

One afternoon while making rounds, I'd met him, curled in a **fetal**

(胎儿的) position. A pale, dried-up old man with a look of death, head half-buried under a blanket. He didn't move when I introduced myself, and he said nothing when I referred to dinner "soon."

At the nurse's station, an attendant provided some history. He had no one. He'd lived too long. Wife of thirty years dead, five sons gone.

Well, maybe I could help. A **chunky**(微胖) but pretty divorced nurse avoiding the male population outside of work, I could satisfy a need. I **flirted**(卖俏).

The next day I wore a dress, not my usual nursing uniform but white. No lights on. Curtains drawn.

Albert shouted at the staff to get out. I pulled a chair close to his bed, crossing my beautiful legs, head **tilted**(倾斜). I gave him a perfect smile.

"Leave me. I want to die."

"What a crime, all us single women out there."

He looked angry. I **rambled on**(漫谈) about how I liked working in "**rehabilitant**" **unit**(康复部门) because I got to watch people reach their maximum **potential**(潜能). It was a place of possibilities. He said nothing.

Two days later during shift report, I learned that Albert had asked when I'd be "on." The charge nurse referred to him as my "boyfriend" and word got around. I never argued. Outside his room, I'd tell others not to bother "my Albert."

Soon he agreed to "**dangle**(悬吊)," sit on the side of the bed to build up sitting tolerance, energy and balance. He agreed to "work" with **physical therapy**(物理疗法) if I'd return "to talk."

Two months later, Albert was on a **walker**(学步器). By the third month, he'd progressed to a cane. Fridays we celebrated **discharges**(出院) with a barbecue. Albert and I danced to Edith Piaf. He wasn't graceful, but he was leading. Tear-streaked cheeks touched as we bade our goodbyes.

Periodically(定期) he would sent roses, **mums**(菊花) and sweet peas to me. He was gardening again.

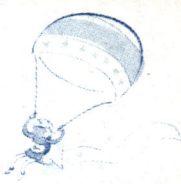

Then one afternoon, a lovely woman came on the unit asking to see "that **hussy**(轻佻女子)."

My **supervisor**(主管) called me; I was in the middle of giving a bed bath.

I came out of the room to meet the woman who wanted to see me.

"So you're the one! The woman who reminded my Albert that he's a man!" said the lovely woman.

Her head tilted in full smile as she handed me a wedding invitation.

92
Christmas Roses

It was the afternoon of December 24, the day before Christmas; and as the newest **hygienist**(健康专家) in our office, I had to work. The only thing that brightened my day was the beautifully decorated Christmas tree in our waiting room and a gift sent to me by a fellow I was dating—a dozen long-stemmed red roses.

As I was cleaning my **operating theatre**(手术室), our receptionist came and said there was a lady in the front office that urgently needed to speak with me. As I stepped out, I noticed a young, tired-looking woman with an infant in her arms.

Nervously, she explained that her husband—a prisoner in a nearby **correctional facility**(劳教所), was my next patient. The guards were scheduled to bring him to the office that afternoon. She told me she wasn't allowed to visit her husband in prison and that he had never seen his son. Her **plea**(请求) was for me to let the boy's father sit in the waiting room with her as long as possible before I called him for his appointment. Since my schedule wasn't full, I agreed. After all, it was Christmas Eve.

A short time later, her husband arrived—with **shackles**(脚镣) on his feet, **cuffs**(手铐) on his hands, and two armed guards as an escort. The woman's tired face lit up like our little Christmas tree when her husband took a seat beside her. I kept peeking out to watch them laugh, cry, and share their child.

After almost an hour, I called the prisoner back to the operating theatre. While I worked, the guards stood just outside my door. The patient seemed like a gentle and humble man. I wondered what he possibly could have done to be held under such conditions. I tried to make him as comfortable as possible.

At the end of the appointment, I wished him a Merry Christmas—a difficult thing to say to a man headed back to prison. He smiled and thanked me. He also said he felt saddened by the fact he hadn't been able to get his wife anything for Christmas. On hearing this, I was inspired with a wonderful idea: I asked him to give my red roses to his wife.

I'll never forget the look on both their faces as the prisoner gave his wife the beautiful, long-stemmed roses. I'm not sure who experienced the most joy—the husband in giving, the wife in receiving, or myself in having the opportunity to share in this special moment.

93

Attitude Is Everything

Jerry was the kind of guy you love to hate. He was always in a good mood and always had something positive to say. When someone would ask him how he was doing, he would reply, "If I were any better, I would be twins!"

He was a unique manager because he had several waiters who had

followed him around from restaurant to restaurant. The reason the waiters followed Jerry was because of his attitude. He was a natural **motivator**(鼓动家). If an employee was having a bad day, Jerry was there telling the employee how to look on the positive side of the situation.

Seeing this really made me curious, so one day I went up to Jerry and asked him, "I don't get it! You can't be a positive person all of the time. How do you do it?"

Jerry replied, "Each morning I wake up and say to myself, 'Jerry, you have two choices today. You can choose to be in a good mood or you can choose to be in a bad mood.' I choose to be in a good mood. Each time something bad happens, I can choose to be a victim or I can choose to learn from it. I choose to learn from it. Every time someone comes to me complaining, I can choose to accept their complaining or I can point out the positive side of life. I choose the positive side of life."

"Yeah, right, it's not that easy," I protested.

"Yes, it is," Jerry said. "Life is all about choices. When you cut away all the junk, every situation is a choice. You choose how you react to situations. You choose how people will affect your mood. You choose to be in a good mood or bad mood. The bottom line: It's your choice how you live life."

I reflected on what Jerry said. Soon thereafter, I left the restaurant industry to start my own business. We lost touch, but often thought about him when I made a choice about life instead of reacting to it.

Several years later, I heard that Jerry did something you are never supposed to do in a restaurant business: he left the back door open one morning and was held up at gunpoint by three armed robbers. While trying to open the **safe**(保险柜), his hand, shaking from nervousness, **slipped off the combination**(拨错了密码). The robbers panicked and shot him. Luckily, Jerry was found relatively quickly and rushed to the local **trauma**(外伤) center. After 18 hours of surgery and weeks of intensive care, Jerry was released from the hospital with **fragments**(碎

片) of the bullets still in his body.

I saw Jerry about six months after the accident. When I asked him how he was, he replied, "If I were any better, I'd be twins. Want to see my scars?"

I declined to see his wounds, but did ask him what had gone through his mind as the robbery took place.

"The first thing that went through my mind was that I should have locked the back door," Jerry replied. "Then, as I lay on the floor, I remembered that I had two choices: I could choose to live, or I could choose to die. I chose to live."

"Weren't you scared? Did you lose consciousness?" I asked.

Jerry continued, "The doctors were great. They kept telling me I was going to be fine. But when they wheeled me into the emergency room and I saw the expressions on the faces of the doctors and nurses, I got really scared. In their eyes, I read, 'He's a dead man.' I knew I needed to take action."

"What did you do?" I asked.

"Well, there was a big, burly nurse shouting questions at me," said Jerry. "She asked if I was **allergic**(过敏) to anything. 'Yes,' I replied. The doctors and nurses stopped working as they waited for my reply... I took a deep breath and yelled, 'Bullets!' Over their laughter, I told them, 'I am choosing to live. Operate on me as if I am alive, not dead.'"

Jerry lived thanks to the skill of his doctors, but also because of his amazing attitude. I learned from him that every day we have the choice to live fully. Attitude, after all, is everything.

94

The Most Beautiful Flower

The park bench was deserted as I sat down to read beneath the long, **straggly**(蔓延的) branches of an old willow tree. I was **disillusioned**(失望) by life with good reason to frown, for the world was intent on dragging me down.

And if that weren't enough to ruin my day, a young boy out of breath approached me, all tired from play. He stood right before me with his head tilted down and said with great excitement, "Look what I found!"

In his hand was a flower, and what a pitiful sight. With its **petals** (花瓣) all worn—not enough rain, or too little light. Wanting him to take his dead flower and go off to play, I **faked**(装出) a small smile and then shifted away.

But instead of **retreating**(退走) he sat next to my side and placed the flower to his nose and declared with surprise, "It sure smells pretty and it's beautiful, too. That's why I picked it. Here, it's for you."

The flower before me was dying or dead. Not **vibrant**(鲜明的) of colors, orange, yellow or red. But I knew I must take it, or he might never leave. So I reached for the flower, and replied, "Just what I need."

But instead of him placing the flower in my hand, he held it mid-air without reason or plan. It was then that I noticed for the very first time, that boy could not see: he was blind.

I heard my voice quiver, tears shone like the sun. I thanked him for picking the very best one.

"You're welcome," he smiled, and then ran off to play, unaware of the impact he'd had on my day.

I sat there and wondered how he managed to see a self-pitying woman beneath an old willow tree. How did he know of my **self-indulged**(自我纵容的) plight? Perhaps from his heart, he'd been blessed with true sight.

Through the eyes of a blind child, at last I could see, the problem was not with the world; the problem was me. And for all of those times I myself had been blind, I **vowed**(发誓) to see beauty, and appreciate every second that's mine.

And then I held that **wilted**(枯萎)flower up to my nose, breathed in the fragrance of a beautiful rose and smiled as that young boy. A flower in his hand is about to change the life of a poor old man.

95

He Never Missed a Game

Bob Richards, the former champion, shared a moving story about a **skinny**(极瘦的) young boy who loved football with all his heart.

Practice after practice, he eagerly gave everything he had. But being half the size of the other boys, he got absolutely nowhere. At all the games, this hopeful **athlete**(运动员) sat on the bench and hardly

ever played.

This teenager lived alone with his father, and the two of them had a very special relationship. Even though the son was always on the bench, his father was always in the stands cheering. He never missed a game. This young man was still the smallest of the class when he entered high school. But his father continued to encourage him but also made it very clear that he did not have to play football if he didn't want to.

But the young man loved football and decided to **hang in**(坚持) there. He was determined to try his best at every practice, and perhaps he'd get to play when he became a senior. All through high school he never missed a practice nor a game but remained a bench-warmer all four years. His faithful father was always in the stands, always with words of encouragement for him. When the young man went to college, he decided to try out for the football team as a "**walk-on**"(临时队员). Everyone was sure he could never **make the cut**(出头), but he did.

The coach admitted that he kept him on the **roster**(名单) because he always put his heart and soul to every practice, and at the same time, provided the other members with the spirit and **hustle**(忙碌) they badly needed.

The news that he had survived the cut thrilled him so much that he rushed to the nearest phone and called his father. His father shared his excitement and was sent season tickets for all the college games. This persistent young athlete never missed practice during his four years at college, but he never got to play in a game.

It was the end of his senior football season, and as he **trotted**(小跑) onto the practice field shortly before the big **playoff**(决赛) game, the coach met him with a telegram. The young man read the telegram and he became deathly silent. Swallowing hard, he mumbled to the coach, "My father died this morning. Is it all right if I miss practice today?"

The coach put his arm gently around his shoulder and said, "Take

215

the rest of the week off, son. And don't even plan to come back to the game on Saturday."

Saturday arrived, and the game was not going well. In the third quarter, when the team was ten points behind, a silent young man quietly slipped into the empty locker room and put on his football **gear**(衣服). As he ran onto the sidelines, the coach and his players were astounded to see their faithful teammate back so soon.

"Coach, please let me play. I've just got to play today," said the young man.

The coach pretended not to hear him. There was no way he wanted his worst player in this close playoff game. But the young man persisted. Finally feeling sorry for the kid, the coach gave in.

"All right," he said. "You can go in."

Before long, the coach, the players and everyone in the stands could not believe their eyes. This little unknown, who had never played before was doing everything right. The opposing team could not stop him. He ran, he passed, blocked, and tackled like a star. His team began to triumph. The score was soon tied. In the closing seconds of the game, this kid **intercepted**(拦截) a pass and ran all the way for the winning **touchdown**(触地得分). They won the game in the end! The fans broke loose. His teammates **hoisted**(举起) him onto their shoulders. Such cheering you never heard.

Finally, after the stands had emptied and the team had showered and left the locker room, the coach noticed that this young man was sitting quietly in the corner all alone. The coach came to him and said, "Kid, I can't believe it. You were **fantastic**(了不起)! Tell me what got into you? How did you do it?"

He looked at the coach, with tears in his eyes, and said, "Well, you knew my Dad died, but did you know that my Dad was blind?" The young man swallowed hard and forced a smile, "Dad came to all my games, but today was the first time he could see me play, and I wanted to show him I could do it!"

96

The House of 1,000 Mirrors

Long ago in a small, far away village, there was a place known as the House of 1,000 Mirrors. A small, happy little dog learned of this place and decided to visit it.

When he arrived, he bounced happily up the stairs to the doorway of the house. He looked through the doorway with his ears lifted high and his tail wagging as fast as it could. To his great surprise, he found himself staring at 1,000 other happy little dogs with their tails wagging just as fast as his. He smiled a great smile, and was answered with 1,000 great smiles just as warm and friendly. As he left the house, he thought to himself, "This is a wonderful place. I will come back and visit it often."

In this same village, another little dog, who was not quite as happy as the first one, decided to visit the house. He slowly climbed the stairs and hung his head low as he looked into the door. When he saw the 1,000 unfriendly looking dogs staring back at him, he **growled** (咆哮) at them and was horrified to see 1,000 little dogs growling back at him. As he left, he thought to himself, "That is a horrible place, and I will never go back there again."

All the faces in the world are mirrors. What kind of reflections do you see in the faces of the people you meet?

97

The Bridge Keeper

There was once a bridge which **spanned**(横跨) a large river. During most of the day the bridge sat with its length running up and down the river paralleled with the banks, allowing ships to pass through freely on both sides of the bridge. But at certain times each day, a train would come along and the bridge would be turned sideways across the river, allowing a train to cross it.

A **switchman**(扳道工) sat in a small **shack**(窝棚) on one side of the river where he operated the controls to turn the bridge and lock it into place as the train crossed. One evening as the switchman was waiting for the last train of the day to come, he looked off into the distance through the dimming twilight and caught sight of the train lights.

He stepped to the control and waited until the train was within a prescribed distance when he was to turn the bridge. He turned the bridge into position, but, to his horror, he found the locking control did not work. If the bridge was not securely in position, it would **wobble**(晃动) back and forth at the ends when the train came onto it, causing the train to jump the track and go crashing into the river. This would be a passenger train with many people aboard.

He left the bridge turned across the river, and hurried across the bridge to the other side of the river where there was a **lever**(操作杆) switch he could hold to operate the lock **manually**(用手工). He would have to hold the lever back firmly as the train crossed. He could hear

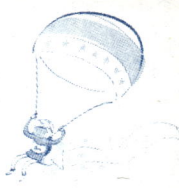

the **rumble**(隆隆声) of the train now, and he took hold of the lever and leaned backward to apply his weight to it, locking the bridge. He kept applying the pressure to keep the mechanism locked. Many lives depended on this man's strength.

Then, coming across the bridge from the direction of his control shack, he heard a sound that made his blood run cold.

"Daddy, where are you?"

His four-year-old son was crossing the bridge to look for him. His first impulse was to cry out to the child, "Run! Run away!" But the train was too close; the tiny legs of the child would never make it across the bridge in time. The man almost left his lever to run and snatch up his son and carry him to safety. But he realized that he could not get back to the lever in time if he helped his son. Either the people on the train or his little son must die. He took a moment to make his decision.

The train passed safely and swiftly on its way, and no one on the train was even aware of the tiny broken body thrown **mercilessly**(无情地) into the river by the onrushing train. Nor were they aware of the pitiful figure of the sobbing man, still clinging tightly to the locking lever long after the train had passed. They did not see him walking home more slowly than he had ever walked: to tell his wife how their son had **brutally**(悲惨地) died.

98

A Goodbye Kiss

The Board Meeting had come to an end. Bob started to stand up and **jostled**(碰到) the table, spilling his coffee over his notes. "How embarrassing. I am getting so clumsy in my old age."

Everyone had a good laugh, and soon we were all telling stories of our most embarrassing moments. It came around to Frank who sat quietly listening to the others. Someone said, "Come on, Frank. Tell us your most embarrassing moment."

Frank laughed and began to tell us of his childhood. "I grew up in San Pedro. My Dad was a fisherman, and he loved the sea. He had his own boat, but it was hard making a living on the sea. He worked hard and would stay out until he caught enough to feed the family. Not just enough for our family, but also for his Mom and Dad and the other kids that were still at home of his Mom and Dad."

He looked at us and said, "I wish you could have met my Dad. He was a big man, and he was strong from pulling the nets and fighting the seas for his catch. When you got close to him, he smelled like the ocean. He would wear his old canvas, foul-weather coat and his **bibbed overalls**(工装裤). His rain hat would be pulled down over his brow. No matter how much my Mother washed them, they would still smell of the sea and of fish."

Frank's voice dropped a bit. "When the weather was bad, he would drive me to school. He had this old truck that he used in his fishing business. That truck was older than he was. It would **wheeze**(喘息) and **rattle**(嘎嘎响) down the road. You could hear it coming for blocks. As he would drive toward the school, I would shrink down into the seat hoping to disappear. Half the time, he would slam to a stop and the old truck would **belch**(冒出) a cloud of smoke. He would pull right up in front, and it seemed like everybody would be standing around and watching. Then he would lean over and give me a big kiss on the cheek and tell me to be a good boy. It was so embarrassing for me. Here, I was twelve years old, and my Dad would lean over and kiss me goodbye!"

He paused and then went on, "I remember the day I decided I was too old for a goodbye kiss. When we got to the school and came to a stop, he had his usual big smile. He started to lean toward me, but I put my hand up and said, 'No, Dad.'

"It was the first time I had ever talked to him that way, and he had this surprised look on his face.

"I said, 'Dad, I'm too old for a goodbye kiss. I'm too old for any kind of kiss.'

"My Dad looked at me for the longest time, and his eyes started to tear up. I had never seen him cry. He turned and looked out the windshield. 'You're right,' he said. 'You are a big boy…a man. I won't kiss you anymore.'"

Frank got a funny look on his face, and the tears began to well up in his eyes, as he spoke. "It wasn't long after that when my Dad went to sea and never came back. It was a day when most of the **fleet**(船队) stayed in, but not Dad. He had a big family to feed. They found his boat **adrift**(漂浮) with its nets half in and half out. He must have gotten into a **gale**(大风) and was trying to save the nets and the floats."

I looked at Frank and saw that tears were running down his cheeks. Frank spoke again. "Guys, you don't know what I would give to have my Dad give me just one more kiss on the cheek… to feel his rough old face… to smell the ocean on him… to feel his arm around my neck. I wish I had been a man then. If I had been a man, I would never have told my Dad I was too old for a goodbye kiss."

99

The Baby Eagle Story

Once upon a time there was a baby eagle living in a nest perched on a cliff overlooking a beautiful valley with waterfalls and streams, trees and lots of little animals, scurrying about enjoying their lives.

The baby eagle liked the nest. It was the only world he had ever known. It was warm and comfortable, had a great view, and even better, he had all the food and love and attention that a great mother eagle could provide. Many times each day the mother would fly down from the sky, land in the nest and feed the baby eagle delicious food. She was like a god to him. He had no idea where she came from or how she worked her magic.

The baby eagle was hungry all the time, but the mother eagle would always come just in time with the food and love and attention he **craved**(渴望). The baby eagle grew strong. His **vision**(视力) grew very sharp. He felt good all the time.

Until one day, the mother stopped coming to the nest.

The baby eagle was hungry.

"I'm sure to die," said the baby eagle, all the time.

"Very soon, death is coming," he cried, with tears streaming down his face. Over and over. But there was no one there to hear him.

Then one day the mother eagle appeared at the top of the mountain cliff, with a big bowl of delicious food and she looked down at her baby. The baby looked up at the mother and cried, "Why did you abandon me? I'm going to die any minute. How could you do this to me?"

The mother said, "Here is some very tasty and nice food. All you have to do is come get it."

"Come get it!" said the baby, with much anger. "How can I go there?"

The mother flew away.

The baby cried and cried and cried.

A few days later, the baby bird was getting more and more hungry.

"I'm going to end it all," he said. "I give up. It is time for me to die."

He didn't know his mother was nearby. She swooped down to the nest with his last meal.

"Eat this, it's your last meal," she said.

The baby cried, but he ate the last meal. The he **whined**(哀诉) and whined about what a bad mother she was.

"You're a terrible mother," he said.

The mother pushed him out of the nest.

He fell.

Head first.

Picked up speed.

Faster and faster.

He screamed.

"I'm dying! I'm dying!" he cried. He picked up more speed.

He looked up at his mother. "How could you do this to me?"

He looked down.

The ground rushed closer, faster and faster. He could **visualize**(想象) his own death so clearly, coming so soon, and cried and whined and complained.

"This isn't fair!" he screamed.

Something strange happens. The air caught behind his arms and they snapped away from his body, with a feeling unlike anything he had ever experienced. He looked down and saw the sky. He wasn't moving towards the ground anymore, his eyes were pointed up at the sun.

"Huh?" he said. "What is going on here!"

"You're flying," his mother said.

"This is fun!" laughed the baby eagle, as he **soared**(翱翔) and dived and **swooped**(俯冲).

"Yes, it is!" said the mother.

100

The Unlocked Door

In Glasgow Scotland, a young girl, like a lot of teens today, got tired of home and the **restraints**(约束) of her parents. The daughter rejected her family's religious lifestyle and said, "I don't want your God. I give up. I'm leaving!"

She left home, deciding to become a woman of the world. Before long, however, she was disappointed and unable to find a job, so she went to the streets to sell her body as a **prostitute**(妓女).

The years passed by, her father died, her mother grew older, and the daughter became more and more stuck to her way of life.

No contact was made between mother and daughter during these years. The mother, having heard of her daughter's **whereabouts**(下落), made her way to the **skid-row section**(平民区) of the city in search of her daughter. She stopped at each of the **rescue missions**(救助站) with a simple request, "Would you allow me to put up this picture on the bulletin board?"

It was a picture of the smiling, gray-haired mother with a handwritten message at the bottom, "I love you still, my dear daughter. Come home!"

Some more months went by, and nothing happened. Then one day the daughter wandered into a rescue mission for a needed meal. She sat absent-mindedly listening to the service music, all the while letting her eyes wander over to the bulletin board. There she saw the picture and thought, "Could that be my mother?"

She couldn't wait until the service music was over. She stood and went to look. It was her mother, and there were those words, "I love you still, my dear daughter. Come home!" As she stood in front of the picture, she wept. It was too good to be true.

By this time it was night, but she was so touched by the message that she started walking home. By the time she arrived, it was early in the morning. She was afraid and made her way **timidly**(羞怯地), not really knowing what to do. As she knocked, the door flew open on its own. She thought some thief must have broken into the house. Concerned for her mother's safety, the young woman ran to the bedroom and found her mother still sleeping. She shook her mother awake and said, "It's me! I'm home!"

The mother couldn't believe her eyes. She wiped her tears and they fell into each other's arms. The daughter said, "I was so worried! The door was open and I thought someone had broken in!"

The mother replied gently, "No, dear. From the day you left, that door has never been locked."

参考文献

1. 董新颖. 心灵阅读(情感篇). 北京：外文出版社，2004.
2. 莫泊桑，著. 莫泊桑中短篇小说全集. 郝运，王振孙译. 上海：上海译文出版社，2006.
3. 王亚男. 心灵阅读(励志篇). 北京：外文出版社，2004.
4. 王燕萍，吴汉梅. 英语夜读365. 武汉：湖北教育出版社，2005.
5. 王颖. 英语奇闻趣事精粹. 北京：世界图书出版公司，1999.
6. 吴颖，邓菲. 白领英语晨读经典365(下). 北京：石油工业出版社，2007.
7. Yang Lili. *Philosophical Stories*. Qingdao Publishing House, 2006.
8. Http：///www. en8848. com. cn/
9. http：//www，enread. com/story/index. html
10. website. informer. com/listen+to+english+story
11. http：//learnenglishkids. britishcouncil. org/en/short-stories
12. www. effortlessenglishpage. com/p/my-story. html
13. http：//www. massreview. org/07submit/htm？gclid = CPHo94yC8akCFQ4RHAodKnBiYA
14. www. cavestory. org/downloads_ game. php
15. www. 4learningenglish. com/
16. cutewriting. blogspot. com/.../short-short-magazines-and-websites
17. www. manythings. org/vos/stories
18. www. good-kids. net/stories/list
19. www. sillybooks. net/

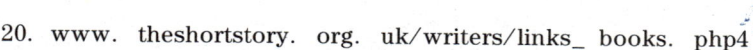

20. www. theshortstory. org. uk/writers/links_ books. php4
21. www. eastoftheweb. com/short-stories/Publishing. html
22. www. valeriemates. com/storysites. html
23. www. litvillage. com
24. www. christiananswers. net/godstory/home. html